CYCLI[ ]
without
TRAFFIC:

THE MIDLANDS
AND PEAK DISTRICT

Nick Cotton

DIAL PRESS

First published 1994

ISBN 0 7110 2287 9

Published by Dial Press
An imprint of Ian Allan Ltd, Terminal House,
Station Approach, Shepperton, Surrey TW17 8AS;

Printed by Ian Allan Printing Ltd, Coombelands House,
Coombelands Lane, Addlestone, Weybridge,
Surrey KT15 1HY.

Publisher's note:
Whilst every effort has been made to ensure the
accuracy of the information contained within this book,
neither Ian Allan Publishing nor the author can accept
any liability arising from the use of the book. In
particular readers will appreciate that only the most
general information regarding open times and
refreshment facilities can be given and intending users
are advised to check prior
to their visit.

Previous Page: *Nick Cotton*
This Page: *Stockfile*

CONTENTS 🚲

For the last five years, bike sales have outnumbered car sales. More and more people are realising that cycling is good for both health and well-being. However, there is still an increasing number of vehicles on the roads which means that even minor lanes can be busy with traffic and potentially dangerous to ride on, particularly with young children.

This book describes 29 easy, waymarked routes where you can cycle away from traffic and gives further information about where else to ride, together with addresses of authorities and organisations which produce cycling leaflets.

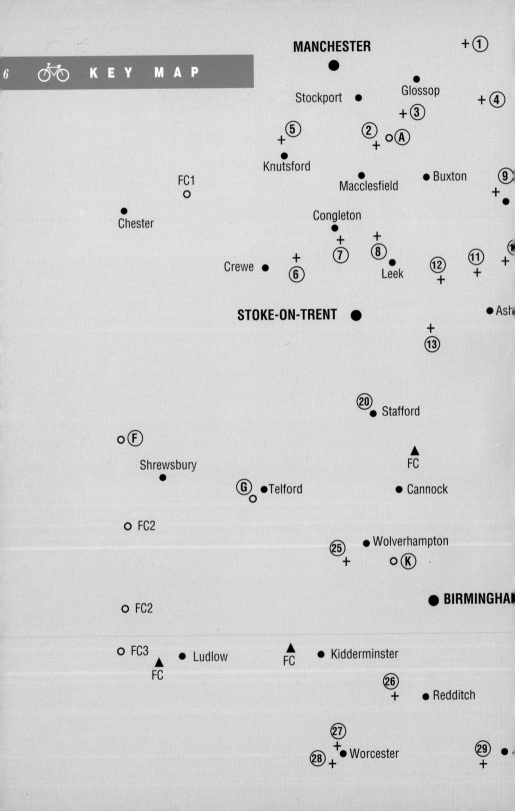

MANCHESTER ●

+ ①

Glossop ●

Stockport ●

+ ④

+ ③

② + ○Ⓐ

+ ⑤
Knutsford ●

● Buxton

⑨
+
●

FC1
○

Chester ●

Congleton ●
+
⑦

+
⑧

Macclesfield ●

⑫
+

⑪
+

Ⓝ

+

Crewe ●
+
⑥

Leek ●

● Ash

STOKE-ON-TRENT ●

+
⑬

⑳
● Stafford

○Ⓕ

Shrewsbury ●

▲
FC

Ⓖ ●Telford
○

● Cannock

○ FC2

㉕
+

● Wolverhampton
○Ⓚ

○ FC2

● BIRMINGHAI

○ FC3

▲
FC

● Ludlow

▲
FC

● Kidderminster

㉖
+

● Redditch

㉗
+

● Worcester

㉘ +

㉙
+

●

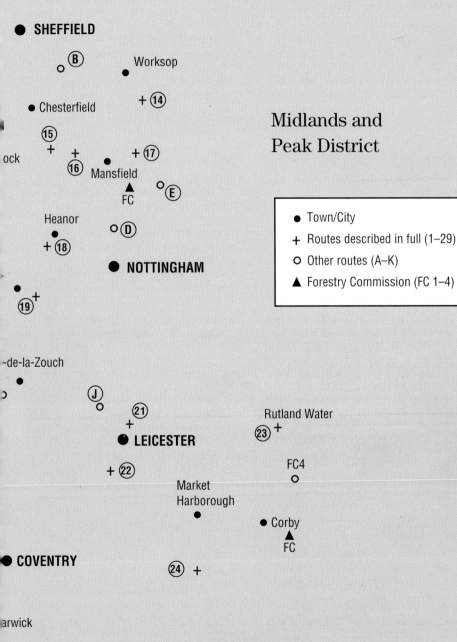

● SHEFFIELD

○ Ⓑ

● Worksop

● Chesterfield

+ ⑭

Ⓜidlands and Peak District

⑮

ock + + ⑯ + ⑰ Mansfield

▲ FC

○ Ⓔ

Heanor ○ Ⓓ
●
+ ⑱

● NOTTINGHAM

●
⑲ +

Midlands and Peak District

● Town/City

+ Routes described in full (1–29)

○ Other routes (A–K)

▲ Forestry Commission (FC 1–4)

-de-la-Zouch
●

）

Ⓙ
○

㉑
+

● LEICESTER

Rutland Water
㉓ +

FC4
○

+ ㉒

Market Harborough
●

● Corby
▲ FC

● COVENTRY

㉔ +

arwick

● NORTHAMPTON

▲ FC

Every attempt has been made to bring together all the trails and areas within the Midlands and Peak District where it is possible to cycle on reasonably flat, good-quality tracks where there are no cars or, in the case of certain country parks, minimal traffic. However, it must be accepted that such a guide can never be fully comprehensive as new developments are continually being implemented as local authorities respond to the demand for the provision of more safe cycle trails.

The trails can be divided into five categories:

1. DISMANTLED RAILWAYS

The vast majority of Britain's railway system was built in the 50 years from 1830 to 1880. After the invention of the car and the development of the road network from the turn of the 20th century onwards, the railways went into decline and in the 1960s many of the lines were closed and the tracks lifted. This was the famous 'Beeching Axe'. It is a great tragedy that Dr Beeching was not a keen leisure cyclist!

Picture: *Stockfile*

Had he set in motion the development of leisure cycle trails along the course of the railways he was so busy closing then we could boast one of the finest recreational cycling networks in the world.

As it is, many of the railways were sold off in small sections to adjacent landowners and the continuity of long sections of dismantled track was lost. Thirty years on, some local authorities (notably the Peak District) have risen to the challenge, seized the opportunity and created some magnificient trails along the course of dismantled railways. Indeed, the High Peak, Tissington and Manifold Trails are some of the very best in the whole country. Other authorities have done absolutely nothing and as time goes by the opportunities for creating trails diminish still further as the land is put to other uses.

To find out what your own authority intends to do in the future about cycle trails in your area, contact the planning department of your county council (see Useful Addresses page 110). Alternatively, if you wish to get involved on a national level, contact Sustrans, 35 King Street, Bristol BS1 4DZ (Tel: 0272 268893), a charity specialising in building cycle tracks.

Dismantled railways make good cycle trails for two reasons. First, the gradients tend to be very gentle, and secondly, the broad stone base is ideal for the top dressing which creates a smooth, firm surface for bicycles. Seventeen of the 29 rides described in this book are along dismantled railways. Some are very short sections of only three miles, but in many cases the local authority has plans to extend them as soon as money becomes available.

2. COUNTRY PARKS

Certain country parks are either big enough to have trails running through them or else the network of the roads within the park has so little traffic (which tends to be slow-moving and highly aware of cyclists) that they have also been included within this guide. The parks tend to have all sorts of other attractions too. At Tatton Park and Clumber Park there is a charge for both the car park and the attractions.

3. FORESTRY COMMISSION LAND

There are four waymarked cycle trails through woodland owned by the Forestry Commission in the area covered by this book, one in each corner of the map.

a. Delamere Forest near Chester

b. Clipstone Forest near Mansfield

c. The Hopton Trail near Ludlow

d. Fineshade Woods near Corby.

Only one of these is described in full in the book (Clipstone Forest — Route 17, p64), but the other trails are very simple to follow.

As a general rule, it is permissible to cycle on the hard forestry tracks in other woodland owned by the Forestry Commission, but there are some exceptions. The chapter on the Forestry Commission (see page 102) gives details of the locations of their sites, and addresses and phone numbers of regional offices so that you can find out the exact regulations (which may change at any time due to logging operations).

4. CANAL TOWPATHS

The British Waterways Board has undertaken a national survey of its 2,000 miles of towpath to see what percentage is suitable for cycling. Unfortunately, the initial results are not very encouraging - only about 10 per cent meet the specified requirements. In certain cases regional waterways boards have co-ordinated with local authorities and the Countryside Commission to improve the towpaths for all users. It is to be hoped that this collaboration continues and extends throughout the country.

Cycling along canal towpaths can provide plenty of interest - wildlife, barges and locks - and the gradient tends to be flat. However, even the best-quality towpaths are not places to cycle fast as they are often busy with anglers and walkers and it is rare that cycling two abreast is feasible.

The chapter on canals (see page 106) gives you a map of the canal network in the Midlands and details of the waterways boards to contact for further information about the towpaths nearest to you.

5. RESERVOIRS

Large reservoirs can sometimes provide excellent cycling opportunities: the rides are circular, the setting is often very beautiful and there is the added attraction of waterfowl to see. Two rides around reservoirs are described in full: one covers the series of reservoirs in the Upper Derwent Valley, which is one of the most spectacular settings of any of the rides in this book. The other is around Rutland Water, which is superbly set up for a full day out with plenty of attractions around the edge of the lake. There is one other reservoir to note in the region, the newest, at Carsington Water between Ashbourne and Matlock. All three reservoirs have bike-hire centres.

OTHER CYCLING ROUTES

If you wish to venture beyond the relatively protected world of cycle trails, there are two choices: write away for leaflets produced by local authorities describing rides on quiet lanes through the

Picture: *Stockfile*

countryside (details are given on page 108), or devise your own route.

Should you choose the second course, study the relevant Ordnance Survey Landranger map: the yellow roads represent the smaller, quieter lanes. When cycling off-road, you must stay on legal rights of way. It is illegal to cycle on footpaths, but you are allowed to use bridleways, byways open to all traffic (BOATs) and roads used as public paths (RUPPs). These are all marked on Ordnance Survey maps. Devising routes 'blind' can sometimes be a bit of a hit-or-miss affair, however. Some tracks may turn out to be very muddy and overgrown, and other hazards include blocked paths, locked gates, and inadequate or non-existent waymarking. If you feel strongly about the condition of a right of way, contact the rights of way department of your local authority and tell them about the problems you have found.

THE COUNTRY CODE

- Enjoy the countryside and respect its life and work.
- Guard against all risk of fire.
- Fasten all gates.
- Keep your dogs under close control.
- Keep to rights of way across farmland.
- Use gates and stiles to cross fences, hedges and walls.
- Leave livestock, crops and machinery alone.
- Take your litter home.
- Help to keep all water clean.
- Protect wildlife, plants and trees.
- Take special care on country roads.
- Make no unnecessary noise.

Bicycles should be thoroughly overhauled on a regular basis but there are certain things worth checking before each ride, and knowledge of how to mend a puncture is essential.

The four most important things to check are:

1. Do both the front and rear brakes work effectively?
2. Are the tyres inflated hard?
3. Is the chain oiled?
4. Is the saddle the right height? (Low enough when sitting in the saddle to be able to touch the ground with your toes, high enough to have your leg almost straight when you are pedalling.)

Other clickings, grindings, gratings, crunchings, rattlings, squeakings, wobblings and rubbings either mean that your bike needs oiling and parts need adjusting, or a trip to your local bike mechanic is long overdue. Try to give a bike shop as much warning as possible; do not expect to turn up and have your bike fixed on the spot.

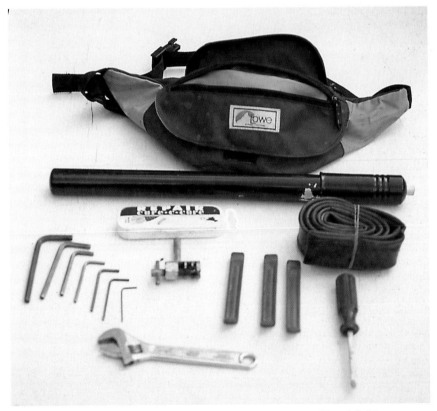

Tool kit - the essentials: pump, repair kit, spare inner tube, allen keys, spanner, screwdriver, chain link remover, tyre lever. Picture: *Nick Cotton*

MENDING A PUNCTURE

You will need:

- a spanner to undo the nuts holding the wheel to the frame
- tyre levers to ease the tyre off the rim
- glue and patches
- a pump

These items should always be carried, even on short rides, as walking with a bike with a flat tyre is not much fun.

1 Remove the wheel which has the puncture, using a spanner to undo the nuts on the hub if it is not fitted with quick-release levers. (You will probably have to unhitch the brake cable in order to remove the wheel.)

2 Remove the tyre from the rim, using tyre levers if the fit is tight. Insert two levers under the rim a few inches apart and push on them together to free the tyre from the rim, taking care not to pinch the inner tube. Work the levers around the rim until the tyre is completely free.

3 Remove the dust cap and any locking ring from the valve. Push the valve inside the tyre then gently pull the inner tube out.

4 Partially inflate the tyre and pass it close to your ear until you hear a hiss (or close to your cheek or lips to feel the escaping air). Locate the puncture and mark it with a cross, using the crayon you should have in the puncture repair kit. (It is not often that you need to use a bucket of water to locate a puncture: you can almost always hear it or feel it.)

5. Deflate the tyre, by pushing in the valve. Hold the tyre so that the section with the puncture is tight over your knuckles. If you have sandpaper in the repair kit, lightly roughen the area around the puncture.

6 Spread glue thinly over the puncture, covering an area slightly larger than the patch you are going to use. Leave to dry for at least five minutes. This is the stage at which many people go wrong: they try to fix the patch too soon. The glue is not an adhesive, it is actually melting the rubber.

7 While waiting for the glue to do its stuff, check the inside of the tyre for any obvious thorn or piece of glass which may have caused the puncture. Run your finger slowly and sensitively around the inside of the tyre to see if you can find the cause of the puncture.

8 After waiting at least five minutes for the glue, select a patch, remove the foil and push the patch firmly into the middle of the gluey area. Peel off the backing paper. If you have a lump of chalk in the repair kit, dust the area with some grated chalk.

9 Replace the tube inside the tyre, starting by pushing the valve through the hole in the rim. Ensure that the tube is completely inside the tyre then using only your hands (ie NOT the tyre levers), gently ease the tyre back inside the rim. The last section will be the hardest, use the heel of the palms of your hands and your thumbs to roll the last part back inside the rim.

10 Re-inflate the tyre, replace the locking ring and the dust cap. Replace the wheel into the frame of the bike and do the nuts up tightly, ensuring that it is set centrally (check by spinning the wheel and seeing if it rubs against the frame). Re-attach the brakes if you have detached the cable.

BICYCLE HIRE

Some of the more popular cycling areas now have bike-hire centres, notably at the large reservoirs and some of the designated Forestry Commission trails. They offer a good opportunity to test different bikes, to give a non-cyclist a chance of trying out cycling, or can save the hassle of loading up and carrying your own bikes to the start of a trail. Wherever cycle-hire centres exist, they are mentioned in the route descriptions in the Essential Information section. It is a good idea to ring beforehand and book a bike, particularly on summer weekends and during the school holidays.

No matter what you do, you'll always get a puncture at some time! Be prepared. *Stockfile*

Comfort, freedom of movement and protection against the unexpected shower should be the three guiding factors in deciding what to wear when you go cycling. Specialist cycling clothing is by no means essential to enjoyable cycling, particularly on the short and easy rides contained in this book.

Starting from the top:

HELMET AND HEADGEAR

The issue of wearing helmets often provokes controversy. Let us hope that it forever remains a matter of personal choice. A helmet does not prevent accidents from happening. Nevertheless, most serious injuries to cyclists are head injuries and helmets can reduce impact.

The case for children wearing helmets is much stronger: they are far more likely to cause damage to themselves by losing control and falling over than an adult. It may be difficult at first to avoid the strap 'pinching' when putting a helmet on a child's head. Bribery of some form or other, once the helmet is securely in place, often helps to persuade the child to see the helmet as a good thing.

In cold weather, a woolly hat or a balaclava is the most effective way of keeping warm. Twenty per cent of body heat is lost through the head.

THE UPPER BODY

It is better to have several thin layers of clothing rather than one thick sweater or coat so that you can make fine adjustments to achieve the most comfortable temperature. Zips or buttons on sleeves and the front of garments also allow you to adjust the temperature.

Try putting your arms right out in front of you - is the clothing tight over your

back? If so, you should wear something a bit looser.

If you are intending to cycle regularly when it is cold, it is worth investing in good-quality thermal underwear and synthetic fleece jackets. These help perspiration to dissipate, do not hold water and dry quickly.

A small woollen scarf and gloves (together with the woolly hat mentioned above) take up very little space and enable you to cope with quite a drop in temperature.

WATERPROOFS

You are far more at risk from exposure on a wet and windy day than a cold, dry day. The biggest danger lies in getting

Picture: *Stockfile*

thoroughly soaked when a strong wind is blowing. Unless you are absolutely certain that it will not rain, it is always worth packing something waterproof. A light, showerproof cagoule takes up little space. If you are buying a waterproof top specifically for cycling, buy a very bright coloured jacket with reflective strips so that you are visible when light is poor.

LEGS

As with the upper body, what you should be looking for is something comfortable which does not restrict your movement. Tight, non-stretch trousers would be the worst thing to wear — uncomfortable at the knees and the hips and full of thick

seams that dig in! Baggy track suit bottoms tend to get caught in the chain and can hold a lot of water if it rains. The best things to wear are leggings or tracksters that are fairly tight at the ankle. However, if you feel reluctant about looking like a ballet dancer, then a long pair of socks worn over the bottom of your trousers keeps them from getting oily or caught in the chain.

CYCLING SHORTS

If you are going to do a lot of cycling then cycling shorts should be the first piece of specialist clothing you buy. They give a lot of padding while allowing your legs to move freely.

FOOTWEAR

Almost any shoe with a reasonably flat sole is appropriate, although you should bear in mind that few of the trails are sealed with tarmac so there may well be puddles or even mud in some cases after rain.

A pair of trainers or old tennis shoes are a good bet.

NB. Take care to ensure that shoe laces are tied and are not dangling where they could get caught in the chain. The same goes for straps on backpacks and straps on panniers, or particularly long scarves!

Picture: *Stockfile*

WHAT TO TAKE

- Hat, scarf, gloves
- Waterproof
- Drink (water or squash is better than fizzy drinks)
- Snacks (fruit, dried fruit, nuts, malt loaf, oatbars)
- Tool kit (pump, puncture repair kit, small adjustable spanner, reversible screwdriver, set of allen keys, tyre levers, chain link extractor)
- Guide book and map (map holder)
- Money
- Camera
- Lock
- Lights and reflective belt (if there is the remotest possibility of being out after dusk)

You can either carry the above in a day-pack on your back or in panniers that fit on to a rack at the rear of the bike. Panniers are the best bet as they do not restrict your movement and do not make your back sweaty.

In theory there are three ways of getting to the start of a ride: cycling there from home; catching a train and cycling to your start point, or carrying the bikes on a car.

If you drive, there are three ways of transporting the bikes:

INSIDE THE CAR

With quick-release skewers now fitted on many new bikes (on the saddle and wheels), it is usually easy to take bikes apart quickly and to fit them into the back of most hatchback cars. If you are carrying more than one bike inside the car you should put an old blanket between each bike to protect paintwork and delicate gear mechanisms from damage.

If you would like to carry your bike(s) inside your car and the idea of quick-release skewers appeals to you, these can normally be fitted by your local bike shop.

Bear in mind that the bikes may be wet and/or muddy when you get back to the car so carry sheets or blankets to protect the upholstery of your car.

ON TOP OF THE CAR

You can buy special roof-racks which fit on top of cars to carry bikes. On some the bikes are carried upside down, others the right way up; on others the right way up with the front wheel removed.

The advantages of this system are that the bikes are kept separate one from the other (ie they do not rub against each other), you can get things out of the boot without problem and they do not obscure visibility.

The disadvantages of this system are that you need to be reasonably tall and strong to lift the bikes up on to the roof, it adds considerably to fuel consumption and feels somewhat precarious in strong crosswinds.

Picture: *Stockfile*

ON THE BACK OF THE CAR

This system seems to be the most versatile and popular method. Different racks can fit almost any sort of car with the use of clips, straps and adjustable angles.

The advantages of this system are that the rack itself folds down to a small space, the rack can be used on a variety of different cars, you do not need to be particularly tall or strong to load bikes on to the rack and fuel consumption is not as badly affected as by bikes on the top.

The disadvantages of this system are that you may well need to buy a separate, hang-on number plate and rear lighting system if the number plate, braking lights and indicators are obscured by the bikes; the bikes are pressed one against the other and may rub off paintwork; you will restrict access to the boot/hatchback.

The deluxe system fits on to the back of a towbar, has its own lighting system and keeps the bikes separate as they fit into individual grooved rails. You can buy systems which hold two, three or four bikes.

GENERAL RULES ABOUT CARRYING BIKES

- Remove all pumps, lights, panniers, water bottles and locks from the bikes before loading them on to the rack.

- Lengths of pipe insulation material are useful for protecting the bikes from rubbing against each other. Try to avoid having delicate parts such as gear mechanisms pushed up against the frame or spokes of the adjoining bike.

- Tie all straps with proper knots. Bows are not good enough.

- Use stretch rubber bungees for extra security, particularly to ensure that the bottom of the bikes is attached to the bumper if you are carrying the bikes on the back of the car.

- If the number plate or brake lights and indicators are obscured you are legally obliged to hang a separate number plate and lights from the back of the bikes.

- It is essential to check and double check all the fixings before setting off and to stop and check again during the course of the journey to ensure nothing has slipped or come loose.

- If you are leaving the bikes on the car for any length of time, lock the bikes to each other and to the rack. While on your ride, it is as well to remove the rack and to lock it inside your car.

Picture: *Stockfile*

BRITISH RAIL

The regulations for carrying bikes on trains seem to change each year and vary from one region to another, one sort of train to another and according to different times of the day and different days of the week. The only advice that can possibly be given that will remain useful is to take nothing for granted and ALWAYS phone British Rail before turning up at the station to find out charges and availability of bike space. Even then you may find that incorrect information is given out: it is always best to go to the station and talk in person to BR station staff.

Network Southeast seems to have adopted a more liberal approach to transporting bikes on trains than other parts of the country and as long as you use common sense (ie avoid rush-hour and do not travel in large groups) then it is often possible to use the train to get to the start of or to return from the finish of a ride. This can be used most successfully on the waterway routes out of London, ie the Grand Union Canal, the Lee Navigation and the Thames Towpath, which all run close to railway lines and to many convenient stations.

THE LONGDENDALE TRAIL
(Northeast of Glossop)

The most recent of the trails that has been opened in this part of the country, the Longdendale Trail follows the course of the old railway from Hadfield to Woodhead.

The route runs along the side of Longdendale past a string of reservoirs lying in the bottom of the valley. The scenery is spectacular, if a little spoilt by the line of pylons that runs parallel with the trail.

Background and places of interest

The Longdendale Trail forms part of the Trans Pennine Trail which will eventually run from Liverpool to Hull, offering a safe, mainly off-road facility for family cycling. Thirty local authorities and the Countryside Commission have been working together since 1988 to create the route and at present (early 1994) just over half has been completed. North West Water purchased the railway line between Hadfield and Woodhead in 1989 and used the ballast in a major engineering project to raise the Woodhead Dam to satisfy current flood safety measures. Once the dam works were complete, demolition and clearance work commenced on the track, followed by major landscaping and drainage works.

The railway through Longdendale provided the first rail link between Manchester and Sheffield. The first passenger train was in 1845. The Woodhead Tunnel was one of the great achievements of the early years of the railway age. After 136 years of operation the line was finally closed in 1981.

The five reservoirs of Bottoms, Valehouse, Rhodeswood, Torside and Woodhead were completed in 1877 and formed the largest artificial expanse of water in the world at the time.

• Glossop

This is two towns in one — an unspoilt 17th-century village with cobbled streets lies next to an industrial 19th-century town with Victorian cotton mills. Near by are the remains of the Roman fort of Ardtolia.

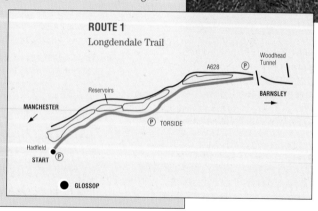

ROUTE 1
Longdendale Trail

Main Picture: *Nick Cotton*

Inset: *Stockfile*

Starting Point: Car park in Padfield. (The trail ends near a car park on the A628, 7 miles east of Hadfield.)

Parking: Turn off the A57 Glossop to Manchester road 2 miles west of Glossop on to Shaw Lane, signposted Hadfield, Padfield. At the Give Way sign at the crossroads at the top of the hill, go straight ahead on to Railway Street. At the T-junction at the bottom of the hill by the Palatine PH turn right; just before the bridge is a car park at the start of the trail.

Distance: 6.5 miles (ie 13 miles round trip).

Map: Ordnance Survey Landranger Sheet 110

or Outdoor Leisure No 1.

Hills: 330-ft climb from the start at Padfield to the end at Woodhead Tunnel.

Surface: Excellent gravel-based track.

Roads and road crossings: The B6105 is crossed once.

Refreshments: Only in Hadfield/Padfield.

Route Instructions:
It is a lot harder to find the start of the trail than to follow it once you have found it! The trail stops at the Woodhead Tunnel entrance 6.5 miles from the start.

THE MIDDLEWOOD WAY
(North of Macclesfield)

Running between Stockport and Macclesfield, the Middlewood Way provides one of the longest stretches of flat, traffic-free cycling close to Greater Manchester. Along much of its length you are riding along a wooded corridor, with occasional views across to the Peak District. The one drawback to this trail is that it has been separated into two lanes, one for horses and one for cyclists and walkers; although this would in theory appear to be a good idea, in practice it means that a good width of the middle of the track is taken up with barriers and vegetation, reducing the usable space for all parties. As a result, it is best avoided after heavy rain or in winter.

Background and places of interest

• Railways and Canals
During the Industrial Revolution, many local industries flourished in this area, especially silk, coal, cotton and stone. Rail and canal links with Stockport were built so that products could be moved more easily. This particular line, the Macclesfield, Bollington and Marple railway, was opened in 1869. As times changed, road transport became cheaper and more popular and these routes were abandoned and left to become derelict and overgrown (this line was closed in 1970). In the early 1980s work was carried out to reopen the routes for recreational use, and the Middlewood Way was opened in 1985.

• Marple
A delightful riverside town in a rocky, wooded ravine. A flight of 16 locks and a triple-arched aqueduct takes the Peak Forest Canal over the River Goyt.

• Lyme Park
(4 miles east of Poynton)
Elegant Elizabethan mansion overlooking a lake and stream, set in extensive gardens within a walled country park with ancient

limes and red and fallow deer. This is also a good place to cycle.

• Adventure playground in Bollington

• Macclesfield
A former silk centre, the last handloom workshop is preserved in Paradise Mill Museum and the history of silk is told in the Heritage Centre. St Michael's Church, reached by its 108 steps, still has its medieval battlements.

• Alderley Edge
(6 miles northwest of Macclesfield)
A wooded escarpment of pink sandstone with superb views of the Cheshire Plain and the Pennines. There are Bronze Age lead and copper mines, and the Wizard Cave, where legendary knights on white horses wait to save the country.

• Jodrell Bank
(10 miles southwest of Macclesfield)
A giant 250ft radio-telescope dish towers above the modern astronomy centre, which includes a planetarium, displays on satellite communications, weather monitoring and working space models. The arboretum has 20,000 trees and shrubs.

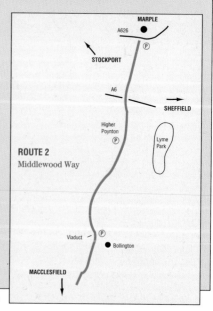

ROUTE 2
Middlewood Way

Right: Interior of Orangery, Lyme Park. *AA Picture Library*

Middlewood Way. OR
the Cycle Hire Centre
at the Adelphi Mill
Gate Lodge on
Grimshaw Lane,
Bollington.

3. Marple. Turn off
the A626 Stockport to
Glossop road in

Starting Points and Parking:

1. Car park by Tesco supermarket just off the roundabout at the start of the A523 dual carriageway to the north of Macclesfield.

2. Adlington Road car park by the viaduct in Bollington, 3 miles northeast of Macclesfield, by the Dog and Partridge PH, signposted

Marple, opposite the Rose Hill Post Office (close to the Railway PH) on to Railway Road, signposted Middlewood Way/Station car park. Look for a sign for the start of the Middlewood Way in the far left-hand corner of the car park.

4. Car parks at Poynton Coppice and Higher

Main Picture: On Alderley Edge. *AA Picture Library*

Inset: *Stockfile*

Poynton, 5 miles southeast of Stockport.

Distance: 11 miles (22 miles round trip).

Map: Ordnance Survey Landranger Sheets 118 and 109.

Hills: None.

Surface: Generally stone-based but the decision to split the path into two with one side for horses and the other for other users has created more problems than it has solved, and there are many muddy sections.

Roads and road crossings: None.

Refreshments: Vale Inn PH, Dog and Partridge PH, Bollington.

Cycle Hire: Cycle hire at Adelphi Mill Gate Lodge, Grimshaw Lane in Bollington. Open 10.00am-6.00pm on weekends from Easter to October and all July and August. Tel: 0625 572681.

Route Instructions:
Unless you live in Macclesfield and can easily arrive by bike at the start of the trail (near the new Tesco supermarket), it is probably best to start a couple of miles north in Bollington, as the section from Macclesfield to Bollington runs alongside a dual carriageway then an ICI factory and, with the exception of a very fine wooden bridge over the main road, is not especially scenic.

THE SETT VALLEY TRAIL

(Between New Mills and Hayfield, south of Glossop)

A short ride along the course of a dismantled railway in the heart of the 19th-century textile country. The ride's best features are in New Mills, with the beautiful rocks and waterfalls of the Torrs Riverside Park and the New Mills Heritage Centre. The views east towards Kinder Scout are also most impressive. The ride could easily be combined with the Middlewood Way between Marple and Macclesfield or the Longdendale Trail to the north of Glossop.

Background and places of interest

The Hayfield Railway line was built for the Midland & Great Central Joint Railway Co and was opened in 1868. Goods trains served all the mills in the Sett Valley, bringing coal and raw materials and taking away finished goods. The railway was closed in 1970.

• Sett Valley Spinning Mills

With the development of water-powered spinning equipment, the banks of the swift and clear running waters of the River Sett were an obvious location for the building of spinning mills, which prospered mightily from the late 18th century through the 19th century.

• The Heritage Centre, New Mills

Exhibition of the town's textile history. Also houses a simulated coal mine and a magnificent model of the town as it was in 1884.

Open 11.00am-4.00pm Tuesday to Friday and 10.30am-4.30pm Saturday and Sunday. Tel: 0663 746904.

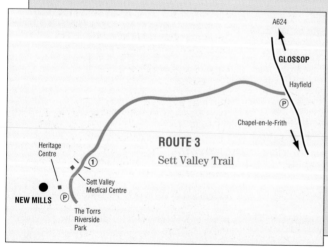

ROUTE 3
Sett Valley Trail

Picture: *Stockfile*

Starting Points:
1. The Sett Valley Visitor Centre in Hayfield.
2. The Sett Valley car park in New Mills.

Parking:
1. Hayfield. Turn off the A624 Glossop to Chapel-en-le-Frith road in Hayfield on to the A6015 to New Mills, then first right on to Wells Road.

2. New Mills. Turn on to Market Street by The Peaks PH in the centre of New Mills, then turn first right, signposted Sett Valley Trail.

Distance: 3 miles (6 miles round trip).

Map: Ordnance Survey Landranger Sheet 110 or Outdoor Leisure No 1.

Hills: One set of steps to negotiate near New Mills.

Surface: Good quality except for the steps mentioned above.

Roads and road crossings: No dangerous crossings.

Refreshments: Hot drinks at the Visitor Centre, Hayfield. Lots of choice in New Mills. The Torrs Riverside Park in New Mills, with its rocks and waterfalls in a spectacular gorge at the confluence of the rivers Goyt and Sett, is a lovely place for a picnic if the weather is fine.

Cycle Hire: Available at Hayfield.
Tel: 0663 746222.

Route Instructions:
1. (Starting from Hayfield). Follow the trail to New Mills. At a T-junction with a road on a hill, with the Sett Valley Medical Centre ahead, turn left then right to continue past the Medical Centre and Leisure Centre. Continue in the same direction under a bridge.

2. Turn left down wooden steps to the wonderful waterfalls, OR turn right up the stone steps for the centre of New Mills and the Heritage Centre.

THE UPPER DERWENT VALLEY
(Between Sheffield and Manchester)

A truly magnificent ride amid the outstanding natural beauty of woodland, lakes and moorland alongside the series of reservoirs in the Upper Derwent Valley. There are various options of single or double circuits or there-and-back rides according to fitness, inclination, weather, type of bicycle and whether you are prepared to spend any time on roads with traffic.

The easiest option would be to follow the road alongside the western edge of Derwent Reservoir and turn back when you felt you had had enough. The most strenuous would be to do a full circuit of all three reservoirs. Take your pick!

Background and nearby places of interest

At the end of the 19th century it was decided that the reservoir needed to supply the nearby cities of Derby, Nottingham, Sheffield and Leicester should be built in the Upper Derwent Valley. Its deep valley with narrow points where dam-building would be relatively easy, high annual rainfall, soft water and a moorland catchment area free from threat of contamination made it an obvious choice. The dams which created the Howden and Derwent Reservoirs were built between 1901 and 1916 and up to 1,000 people lived in the self-contained workers' village at Birchinlee. The third dam, to create the Ladybower Reservoir, was built between 1935 and 1945.

Severn Trent Water works closely with several regional and national bodies to help conserve and maintain the 3,700 acres of water and woods in its care. It was given a Centre of Excellence Award in 1992. Protection is provided for rare native birds such as the goshawk, crossbill and common sandpiper. One man has been given the task of reconstructing 56 miles of drystone walling. At a mile a year, he reckons he will be finished in about the year 2043!

• The Dambusters Raid

In the weeks leading up to the famous raid on Germany in 1943, Derwent Water was frequently used for flight practice by the 617 Squadron, as the topography of the dams was similar to the targets in Germany.

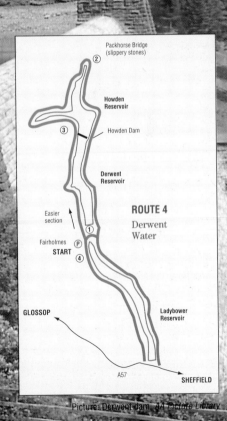

Packhorse Bridge
(slippery stones)

②

Howden
Reservoir

③

Howden Dam

Derwent
Reservoir

ROUTE 4
Derwent
Water

Easier
section

①

Fairholmes ℗
START

④

Ladybower
Reservoir

GLOSSOP

A57

SHEFFIELD

Picture: Derwent dam. *AA Picture Library*

Starting Point: The Visitor Centre at the top end of Ladybower Reservoir (Fairholmes).

Parking: Turn off the A57 Sheffield to Glossop road just by the west side of the viaduct over Ladybower Reservoir. Continue for 2.5 miles to the car park at the Visitor Centre.

Distance: Two loops, of 11 miles and 5 miles. The upper loop (11 miles), around Derwent and Howden Reservoirs, is not only longer but also runs over rougher terrain at the far northeast section of the ride. An easier alternative would be to go out and back on the road that runs along the west side of the lakes.

Map: Ordnance Survey Landranger Sheet 110 or Outdoor Leisure No 1.

Hills: Several small climbs. The packhorse bridge at Slippery Stones is 270ft higher than the Visitor Centre.

Surface: Varies from tarmac to stone/gravel forestry track to a rougher track on the eastern side of the Howden Reservoir (mountain bikes are preferable for this section).

Roads and road crossings: Vehicles are allowed to use the road on the western side of the Derwent and Howden Reservoirs during the week but not at the weekends. There is traffic on the road from the A57 up to the Visitor Centre, but there is also a pavement.

Refreshments: Hot drinks, cakes and sweets available at the Visitor Centre.

Above: Ladybower Reservoir. *AA Picture Library*

Cycle Hire: Available at Fairholmes Visitor Centre. Tel: 0433 651261.

Route Instructions:
(for the full circuit, starting with the upper lakes)

1. From the Visitor Centre, cross to the other side of the reservoir via the bridge, signposted 'No access. Road closed except for access to premises and disabled'. Follow the tarmac past the dam and away from the dam for 300yds, climbing a hill. After a short stone wall, turn left sharply back on yourself on to a broad track.

2. Follow this broad stone track for 4.5 miles until you see a stone bridge down to your left, signposted 'Westendal/Portcastles/Hope Woodlands via Packhorse Bridge'. Cross the bridge.

3. Follow the road back alongside the reservoirs. You will descend to cross each 'arm' of the reservoir and climb again after each crossing.

4. At the Visitor Centre, you may wish to do a second loop, in which case continue along the road down to the A57, turn left on to the viaduct (use pavement), then 50yds past the end of the bridge, turn sharp left on to a tarmac track marked Public Bridleway.

5. Follow this back to the start, following the road beneath the dam.

Right: Ladybower Reservoir. *Mike Williams*

ALTRINCHAM

Main entrance

Park boundary

A556

Ⓟ Ⓟ Mansion

Old Hall

Garden

Ⓟ

A50

Ⓟ

Lake

ROUTE 5

Tatton Park

Ⓟ

Knutsford Entrance

KNUTSFORD ⬤

Picture: The Japanese Garden, Tatton Park. *AA Picture Library*

Starting Point: The main car park, Tatton Park.

Parking: Follow signs off the A556 between Junction 7/8 of the M56 and Junction 19 of the M6 between Altrincham and Knutsford.

Distance: There are some 8 miles of roads in the park. It is suggested that you explore wherever takes your fancy, staying on the surfaced roads.

Map: Ordnance Survey Landranger Sheets 109 and 118, although the map provided by the park is of more use.

Hills: Gently undulating.

Surface: All tarmac.

Roads and road crossings: The route is all on the estate's roads, so there will be traffic, but it

TATTON PARK
(North of Knutsford)

Tatton is a complete country estate, with mansion, farm, gardens and parkland. Exploring it by bike is one of the best ways of taking it all in. The parkland has been a refuge for deer for 10,000 years and many of these animals can be seen on your way through the park.

Background and places of interest

• Tatton Park
The sumptuous 18th-century mansion appeared in the television version of Brideshead Revisited. The park is open 10.30am-6.30pm Tuesday to Sunday. Opening times for the mansion and other attractions vary during the year. Pedestrians and cyclists are allowed in free. Visit the farm, the old hall and the mansion. There is also a restaurant, shops and a children's playground (family tickets available for combined admission to all attractions). Tel: 0565 750250 or 654822.

• The Old Hall
A guided tour through 500 years of history, from the smoky shadows of medieval England through a sunlit Stuart bedchamber to a gamekeeper's cosy parlour.

• Home Farm
The wealth of Tatton Hall was based on agriculture. Farming methods and original breeds of animals provide a picture of the past. At the stables the vital role of the horse on a country estate is brought to life.

• The Mansion
Majestic staterooms and richly appointed family quarters house the finest furniture and works of art. In stark contrast, the humble and hard life of of the servant is seen 'below stairs'.

• The Gardens and Deer Park
Exotic specimens collected from around the world, including the Japanese gardens and banks of azaleas. All this set amid 1,000 acres of woodland, water and wildlife.

is travelling slowly and signs tell motorists to be aware of cyclists. As might be expected, there will be more traffic during weekends in summer, so try to plan accordingly, visiting the park during the week or out of season.

Refreshments: Restaurant and refreshments near the mansion.

Cycle Hire: In Tatton Park, in the courtyard opposite the restaurant. Open at weekends from mid-April to September 10.30am-6.00pm and every day during July and August.
Tel: 0625 572681.

Route Instructions:
As pointed out under the 'Distance' section, it is suggested that you explore wherever takes your fancy, as long as you stay on the surfaced roads.

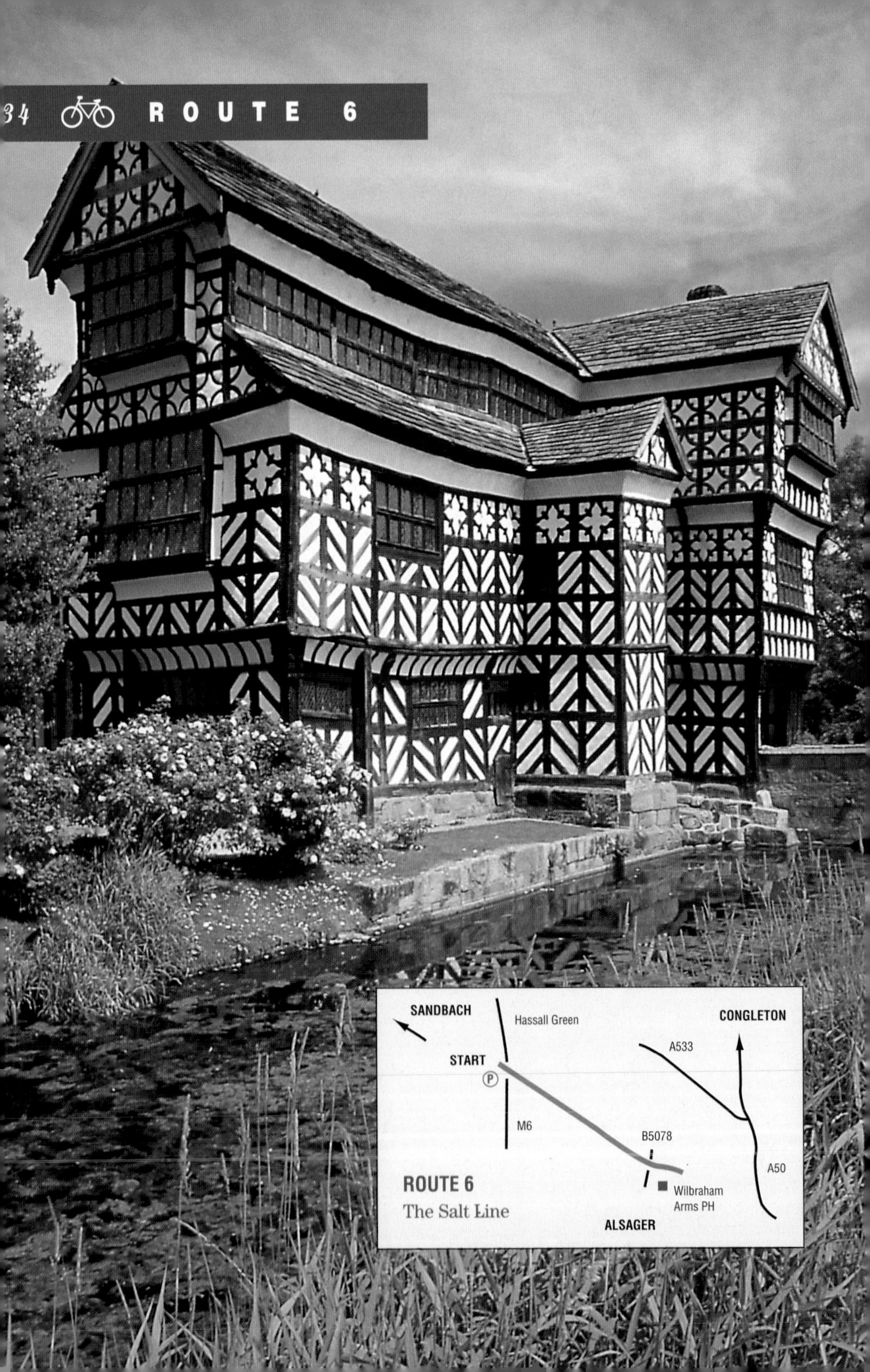

ROUTE 6
The Salt Line

SANDBACH   Hassall Green   CONGLETON

START   A533

M6   B5078

                                        A50
                              Wilbraham
                              Arms PH
ALSAGER

THE SALT LINE

(From Hassall Green to Alsager, northwest of Stoke)

A short, well-maintained stretch of dismantled railway through attractive woodland, with a good family pub at the end of the ride. It could easily be combined with either the Congleton to Biddulph ride or the Rudyard Lake to Leek ride.

Background and places of interest

The railway was built by the North Staffordshire Railway Company in 1858 with the primary function of carrying minerals to and from Stoke-on-Trent. The Trent and Mersey Canal proved vital in the construction of the line as many of the bulky materials were transported by narrowboat. The line began as goods only, expanded to take passengers, then reverted to goods only between 1930 and 1970 when it finally closed. The old course of the railway is rich in species of flowers, birds and butterflies.

- **Little Moreton Hall**
  (3 miles northeast of Alsager, just off the A34)
  A dazzling jigsaw of black timber and white plaster. Built in the 15th century within a moat, it has leaning walls, elegant gables and windows and a 68ft Long Gallery. Fine wall paintings, plus herb and knot gardens.

Starting Point: Car park just beneath the M6 between Hassall Green and Wheelock Heath, 1 mile off the A533 Alsager to Sandbach road.

Parking: Turn off the A533 2.5 miles southeast of Sandbach opposite the New Inn PH on to New Inn Lane, signposted 'Hassall Green ½/Wheelock 3'. Go under the motorway and take the first right into the car park.

Distance: 2.5 miles (5 miles round trip).

Map: Ordnance Survey Landranger Sheet 118.

Hills: None.

Surface: Good gravel-based track.

Roads and road crossings: The B5078 is crossed at Lawton Heath End. If you decide to go to the pubs at either end of the trail there are short road sections.

Refreshments: Wilbraham Arms PH, 200yds beyond the end of the trail towards Alsager. Lockside Cafe and Romping Donkey PH in Hassall Green, 0.5 mile from start.

Route Instructions:
(Starting from the Hassall Green end.) At the second road (the B5078) go straight ahead on to Cherry Lane then turn right as soon as possible to rejoin the course of the old railway (it stops fairly abruptly after a further 0.75 mile). Alternatively, at the B5078, turn right for 200yds to go to the Wilbraham Arms PH.

Main Picture: Little Moreton Hall. *AA Picture Library*

Above: *Stockfile*

THE BIDDULPH VALLEY TRAIL

(Along the dismantled Biddulph Valley Railway)

Although the start to the ride is not as convenient as most, with no designated car park, this trail along the dismantled railway of the Biddulph Valley line is nevertheless most rewarding, with the raised track bed providing fine views across to the Peak District. The ride passes through woodland and beneath a magnificent viaduct near Congleton.

Background and places of interest

The Biddulph Valley line was opened in 1859. As Congleton's main arterial link with the Potteries, it provided the town's economic lifeblood with the movement of freight of every description from straw to war weapons. It lasted 109 years and the final train ran on 1 April 1968.

In 1980, Congleton Borough Council bought the line from British Rail and the line was put into service once again to provide recreation for local people and a refuge for wildlife.

- **Biddulph Grange Garden**
  (just off the A527 to the north of Biddulph)
  A unique 15-acre Victorian garden with an Egyptian court, Chinese pagoda, Willow Pattern bridge and pinetum.
  Open April to October Wednesday to Sunday 12.00-6.00pm. November/December weekends only. Tel: 0782 517999.

Starting Points:

1. Congleton. The track/lane to the right of Brunswick Wharf Depot (owned by Congleton Borough Council) opposite Brook Street Garage and petrol station, 0.5 mile out of Congleton on the A54 Buxton road.

2. Biddulph. At the traffic lights at the southern end of Biddulph on the A527 Congleton to Stoke road, turn right, signposted Mow Cop/Brown Lees. The trail starts beneath the railway bridge after 200yds.

Parking:

1. Congleton. No specific nearby car park. Use the adjacent streets with consideration, using your discretion.

2. Biddulph. A similar story. Park with consideration.

Distance: 5 miles (10 miles round trip).

Map: Ordnance Survey Landranger Sheet 118.

Hills: None.

Surface: Stone-based track but some muddy

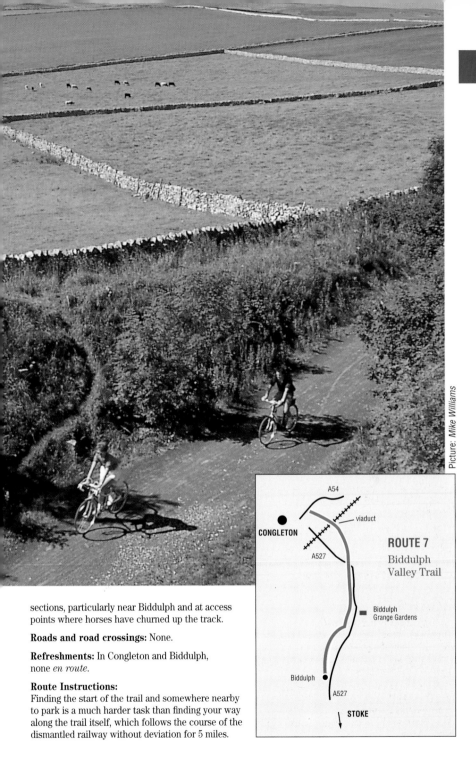

ROUTE 7
Biddulph Valley Trail

CONGLETON

A54

viaduct

A527

Biddulph Grange Gardens

Biddulph

A527

STOKE

sections, particularly near Biddulph and at access points where horses have churned up the track.

Roads and road crossings: None.

Refreshments: In Congleton and Biddulph, none *en route*.

Route Instructions:
Finding the start of the trail and somewhere nearby to park is a much harder task than finding your way along the trail itself, which follows the course of the dismantled railway without deviation for 5 miles.

NORTH AND SOUTH FROM RUDYARD LAKE (NEAR LEEK)

The ride alongside Rudyard Lake is a real delight, with colourful yachts and dinghies set against a background of steep wooded slopes. The quality of the trail does vary, however, the best section being closest to the lake; what lies north of the lake towards Rushton Spencer is narrower and, after rain, muddier.

Background and places of interest

The young Kiplings spent their courting days here and were so enamoured of the place that they named their first son, Rudyard, after the area. Rudyard Lake is a feeder reservoir for the Caldon Canal. It was a very popular Victorian resort with hundreds of holiday-makers arriving by train during the season.

- **Cheddleton Railway Centre, south of Leek**
  Display of locomotives, a relic museum, a souvenir shop and refreshments.
  Open on Sundays throughout the year. Rides on steam engines on summer Sundays. Tel: 0538 360522.

- **Brindley Mill and Museum, Leek**
  This restored water-powered corn mill built by James Brindley illustrates the life and times of the great canal builder.
  Open on Saturdays and Sundays Easter to end of October. Tel: 0538 381000.

- **Moorlands Farm Park, Ipstones Edge**
  (5 miles southeast of Leek)
  Over 70 British rare breeds and domestic animals. Also a pets' corner, a children's play area, a souvenir shop, a picnic area and refreshments. Magnificent views.
  Open 10.30am to dusk, April to November. Tel: 0538 266479.

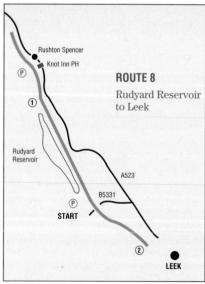

ROUTE 8
Rudyard Reservoir to Leek

Rushton Spencer
Knot Inn PH
Ⓟ
①
Rudyard Reservoir
A523
B5331
Ⓟ
START
②
LEEK

Main Picture: Rudyard reservoir. *AA Picture Library*

Starting Point: The car park at the southern end of Rudyard Lake, 3 miles northwest of Leek.

Parking: Turn off the A523 Leek to Macclesfield road 2 miles northwest of Leek on to the B5331, signposted 'Rudyard Lake'. Just after going under a railway bridge, turn immediately left into the car park.

Distance: 3 miles north to the Knot Inn PH at Rushton Spencer (6 miles round trip), 1.5 miles south to the outskirts of Leek (3 miles round trip).

Map: Ordnance Survey Landranger Sheet 118.

Hills: None.

Surface: In general stone-based. Some muddy stretches on the northern section. The track is at its widest and best near the reservoir.

Roads and road crossings: None.

Refreshments: Knot Inn PH at the north end of the ride (Rushton Spencer).

Cycle Hire: At Rudyard Lake Visitor Centre. Tel: 0538 33280.

Route Instructions:

1. (Heading north) Follow the broad track alongside the eastern side of the lake. At the end of the lake, shortly after going under a bridge, you will come to a wide parking area. Continue in the same direction for 150yds, keeping an eye out for a Highways Act 1959 sign. At this point, turn right and join a parallel track to continue in the same direction. (This section can get muddy.)

2. (Heading south) The trail ends on the outskirts of Leek near a large field.

Inset: *Stockfile*

THE MONSAL TRAIL

(North of Bakewell)

The Monsal Trail, running along the course of a dismantled railway, passes through some of the most beautiful countryside in the southern Peak District. A short section of the trail is open to cyclists.

Background and places of interest

In 1863 the railway link between Rowsley (north of Matlock) and Manchester was completed and the Midland Railway achieved its ambition of having its own London to Manchester mainline route. Coal was unloaded at Bakewell Station and delivered to remote areas, while milk churns from surrounding farms were sent to London. Closure of the Peak section of the line occurred in 1968. After 12 years of negotiation, the Peak National Park authority finally persuaded British Rail to allow them to turn it into a recreational trail. Only the eastern section from Coombs Road Viaduct to Longstone is open to bicycles.

- **Haddon Hall, Bakewell**
  (1.5 miles south of Bakewell on the A6)
  The Derbyshire seat of the Duke of Rutland, Haddon Hall is everybody's idea of a perfect English country house - a totally unspoilt medieval and Tudor manor house with magnificent terraced rose gardens.

  Open April to September. Closed on Mondays (and Sundays in July and August). Tel: 0629 812855.

- **Chatsworth House, Bakewell**
  (3 miles east of Bakewell)
  Home of the Duke and Duchess of Devonshire and one of England's most beautiful and best loved houses in a splendid setting on the banks of the River Derwent. Large gardens with cascade and fountains. Chatsworth Farmyard and Adventure Playground

  Open daily from end of March to end of October. Tel: 0246 582204.

Picture: Chatsworth House. *AA Picture Library*

Picture: Haddon Hall. *AA Picture Library*

Starting Point: Coombs Road car park in Bakewell.

Parking: From the centre of Bakewell take the A619 towards Chesterfield. Immediately after crossing the bridge over the River Wye, turn first right on to Station Road, then right again on to Coombs Road.

Distance: 5 miles (10 miles round trip).

Map: Ordnance Survey Landranger Sheet 119 or Outdoor Leisure No 24 'White Peak Area'.

Hills: None.

Surface: Good, broad, stone-based track.

Roads and road crossings: The ride starts with a short section on a No Through Road with almost no traffic. You will need to use quiet lanes for less than a mile to get to the pubs.

Refreshments:
Teas and coffees at The County Bookshop in the old station a mile north of Bakewell. Open 9am-5pm Monday to Friday, 10.30am-5.15pm Saturday, 11.00am-5.15pm Sunday.

Two pubs just off the route (exit via the steps at Thornbridge Hall):

The Crispin PH, Great Longstone

The Pack Horse Inn, Little Longstone

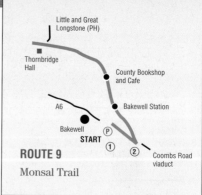

ROUTE 9

Monsal Trail

NB. Although the Monsal Trail is much longer than 5 miles, this is the only section open to cyclists.

Route Instructions:
1. From the car park, turn right along the lane (away from Bakewell) for 0.75 mile. Shortly after passing Adelaide House on your right, at the start of the woodland just before the railway bridge, turn left by a wooden gate and go steeply uphill to join the track.

2. Turn left on the track and continue for 4 miles to its end.

THE HIGH PEAK TRAIL
(West of Matlock)

Along with the Tissington Trail, the High Peak Trail must rate as one of the best cycling trails in the country. They are both superbly maintained scenic routes though the limestone countryside of the White Peak. The easiest section lies between Parsley Hay and Middleton Top and there are fabulous views all along this stretch. If all local authorities and National Parks in the country were to show the vision and initiative of those involved in the Peak District, Britain would have a leisure cycling network to show off to the rest of the world.

Picture: Arkwright Mill, Cromford. *AA Picture Library*

Background and nearby places of interest

• The Cromford & High Peak Railway
One of the earliest railways in the country, the original idea was to link the Cromford Canal to the Peak Forest Canal at Whaley Bridge. However, as numerous engineering difficulties faced the canal designers, it was decided to use the new railway technology as a more efficient solution to the problem. Instead of locks, the engineers used steep inclines, each worked by a steam-powered engine to haul the wagons up the gradients.

The 33-mile line was constructed by Josiah Jessop. It took five years to build and was opened in 1830. The line was used mainly for transporting lime, limestone and agricultural products. In the early days, horses were used to haul the wagons along the rails. Halts were called 'wharfs' after the old canal name. The line remained an integral part of the canal system until 1853, when a connection to the rapidly expanding railway network changed its function to a branch line serving local needs.

When the line's profitability began to decline and maintenance costs continued to rise, closure became inevitable. This happened to the final section from Friden Wharf to Parsley Hay in 1967.

• High Peak Junction Workshops, Cromford
Original workshops of the Cromford and High Peak Railway.

Open every weekend from Easter to mid-September.

• The Middleton Top Engine House
Originally built to haul wagons up the 1-in-9 gradient of the Middleton Incline, the Middleton Engine worked for 134 years before its retirement in 1963. Restored by volunteers, the engine is now open to the public between Easter and October on Sundays, 10.30am-5.00pm and can be seen in motion on the first weekend in each month.

• The Roystone Grange Trail (near Minninglow)
Guides you through a landscape of remains dating back to the Bronze Age, Roman times and the Middle Ages.

• National Stone Centre
(Porter Lane, Wirksworth)
This indoor exhibition tells the 'Story of Stone' in Britain from prehistoric axe factories to hi-tech processing, including how stone is formed and environmental issues.

Open daily 10.00am-4.00pm October to March, 10.00am-5.00pm April to September.

• Drystone Walls
In the late Middle Ages agriculture became dominated by livestock-farming and numerous monastic farms (granges) were established in the area which kept sheep to supply the country's thriving wool trade. The majority of the walls were built between 1760 and 1830 following the passing of the Enclosure Acts.

Best Starting Points:
1. Middleton Top, 4 miles southwest of Matlock on the B5035 road towards Ashbourne.

2. Parsley Hay, on the A515 halfway between Ashbourne and Buxton.

Parking:
As above and also:

1. High Peak Junction (southeast of Cromford)

2. Black Rocks (southwest of Cromford)

3. Friden (just north of the A515/A5012 junction)

4. Sparklow (just west of Monyash, near the A515/B5055 junction)

Distance: 17.5 miles from High Peak Junction, near Cromford to Dowlow, near Buxton (35 mile round trip). The best, flattest section is the 12-mile stretch between Middleton Top and Parsley Hay.

Picture: *Stockfile*

Maps: Ordnance Survey Landranger Sheet 119 or Outdoor Leisure 24.

Hills: The trail maintains a fairly steady height between Middleton Top and Sparklow but southeast of Middleton Top the trail loses height via two long steep hills down to High Peak Junction (ie there is a drop of some 900ft down to the valley floor).

Surface: Excellent, broad, stone- and gravel-based track.

Roads and road crossings: The A5012 must be crossed close to Friden.

Refreshments: Royal Oak PH, Hurdlow (Sparklow).

Hot and cold drinks at Middleton Top and Parsley Hay.

Cycle Hire: Available at Parsley Hay (Tel: 0298 84493) and Middleton Top (Tel: 0629 823204). Also at Ashbourne should you wish to combine the High Peak and Tissington Trail (Tel: 0335 43156).

Route Instructions:
Once you have chosen your starting point it is impossible to get lost on the High Peak Trail. As mentioned in the 'Distance' section, the best, flattest section is the 12-mile stretch between Middleton Top and Parsley Hay. Remember there is a 900ft drop from Middleton Top down towards Matlock, which is great fun going down if you have good brakes but a very tough challenge to cycle up.

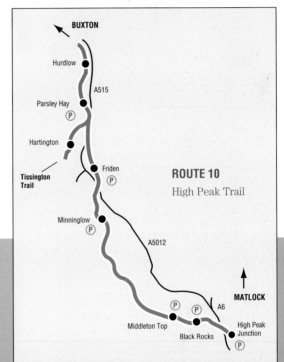

ROUTE 10

High Peak Trail

Picture: Parsley Hay. *Mike Williams*

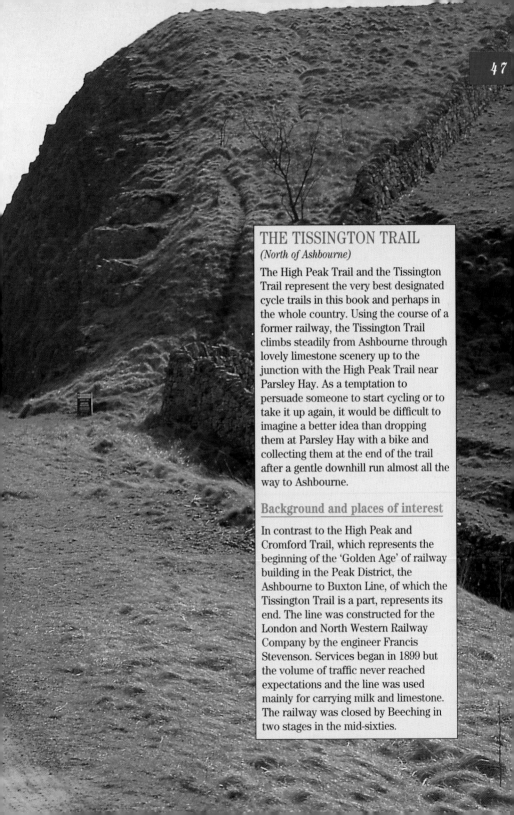

THE TISSINGTON TRAIL
(North of Ashbourne)

The High Peak Trail and the Tissington Trail represent the very best designated cycle trails in this book and perhaps in the whole country. Using the course of a former railway, the Tissington Trail climbs steadily from Ashbourne through lovely limestone scenery up to the junction with the High Peak Trail near Parsley Hay. As a temptation to persuade someone to start cycling or to take it up again, it would be difficult to imagine a better idea than dropping them at Parsley Hay with a bike and collecting them at the end of the trail after a gentle downhill run almost all the way to Ashbourne.

Background and places of interest

In contrast to the High Peak and Cromford Trail, which represents the beginning of the 'Golden Age' of railway building in the Peak District, the Ashbourne to Buxton Line, of which the Tissington Trail is a part, represents its end. The line was constructed for the London and North Western Railway Company by the engineer Francis Stevenson. Services began in 1899 but the volume of traffic never reached expectations and the line was used mainly for carrying milk and limestone. The railway was closed by Beeching in two stages in the mid-sixties.

Starting Points: The trail runs from the west of Ashbourne to its junction with the High Peak Trail near Parsley Hay on the A515 south of Monyash. There is a height difference of almost 750ft from Ashbourne up to Parsley Hay, so it is best to start from Ashbourne while you are fresh and leave yourself with a downhill run for the second half of the ride.

Parking: From the Tourist Information Centre in the centre of Ashbourne, take the A515 north towards Buxton. Turn first left, then on a sharp right-hand bend, on a steep hill, bear left signposted Mapleton/Okeover/Tissington Trail.

Distance: 13 miles (26 miles round trip).

Map: Ordnance Survey Landranger Sheet 119 or Outdoor Leisure No 24 (the 2-mile section closest to Ashbourne is not covered by the Outdoor Leisure map).

Hills: A steady 750ft climb from Ashbourne to Parsley Hay (or a gentle 750ft descent if you can persuade someone to drop you at the top at Parsley Hay and collect you at the bottom at Ashbourne).

Surface: Excellent surface throughout.

Roads and road crossings: None.

Refreshments: Soft drinks and sweets at Parsley Hay and Tissington. Pubs just off the route in Thorpe and Biggin.

Cycle Hire: Mapleton Lane, Ashbourne.
Tel: 0335 43156. Parsley Hay, just off the A515 between Buxton and Ashbourne.
Tel: 0298 484493.

Route Instructions:
As explained in the Starting Points' and 'Hills' sections, if you are intending to do a 'there and back' ride it is best to start from Ashbourne and climb while you are fresh and full of energy, leaving the descent for the second half of the ride. The trail is easy to follow and it is impossible to get lost.

Main Picture: Parsley Hay. *Mike Williams*

Inset above: *Mike Williams*

BUXTON

A515

Parsley Hay
(P)

High Peak
Trail

Hartington
(P)

ROUTE 11
Tissington Trail

Alsop
(P)

Tissington
(P)

(P) Thorpe

(P)
Mapleton Lane

ASHBOURNE

Inset above: *Mike Williams*

THE MANIFOLD TRAIL

(Northwest of Ashbourne)

One of the best trails in the area, it runs along the course of a dismantled railway line, following the course of two rivers, the Manifold and the Hamps.

The Manifold appears and disappears: during the drier months it takes an underground course, leaving just the dry, stony river bed and tree-lined banks. High above the wooded hillsides are accessible caves.

Background and places of interest

The Leek & Manifold Valley Light Railway was opened in 1904, closed in 1934 and converted to recreational use in 1937. It was a narrow-gauge railway designed by E. R. Calthrop who had tested and proved his ideas on the Barsi Light Railway in India.

• Thor's Cave
Many objects have been found in the cave, proving man has occupied this site for long periods in the past.

• River Manifold
Near Thor's Cave the river disappears underground for 5 miles, re-emerging at Ilam.

• Blackbrook World of Birds, Winkhill
(2 miles northwest of Waterhouses, just off the A523 behind the Little Chef)
A large collection of wildfowl and domestic waterfowl and many unusual birds. Children's farm and pets' corner with baby animals often on view. Gift shop, information area and art gallery. Picnic areas around the grounds.

Open daily 12.00-6.00pm, Easter to the end of October. Tel: 0538 266486.

• Moorlands Farm Park, Ipstones Edge
(3 miles west of Waterhouses)

(See page 38)

Picture: Thor's Cave. AA Picture Library.

Picture below: *Mike Williams*

junction of the rivers Hamps and Manifold, south to the road at Waterhouses.

Surface: Excellent condition throughout.

Roads and road crossings: The Manifold Way uses a section of a quiet lane for about 1.5 miles. Care should be taken at the southern end of the trail when crossing the A523. (This is not necessary if you start at Hulme End.)

Refreshments:

The Manifold Valley PH at Hulme End. Various tea shops and refreshment vans along the way. Ye Olde Crown PH at Waterhouses.

ROUTE 12
Manifold Trail

Hulme End
B5054
River Manifold
Wetton Mill
Thors Cave
River Manifold
River Hamps
LEEK
Waterhouses
A523
ASHBOURNE

Starting Points:

1. Hulme End, on the B5054 15 miles southwest of Bakewell.

2. Waterhouses, on the A523 between Leek and Ashbourne.

Parking:

1. There is a car park off the B5054 in Hulme End, just to the west of the Manifold Valley PH. The Manifold Way starts from this car park.

2. To find the car park in Waterhouses, turn off the A523 Leek to Ashbourne road at Ye Olde Crown Hotel in Waterhouses, signposted 'Cauldon Lowe 2.5/Cheadle 9/Manifold Track'. Go under the bridge and immediately left into the car park.
To get to the start of the trail, go to the far end of the car park and follow the arrows which direct you back on yourself underneath a railway bridge and on to the road. Cross the road with care, turn right and either walk along the pavement for 400yds or cycle on the road to the well-signposted start.

Distance: 8 miles (16 miles round trip).

Map: Ordnance Survey Landranger Sheet 119 or Outdoor Leisure No 24.

Hills: There is a gentle 180ft climb from the

Cycle Hire:

1. Brown End Farm Cycle Hire at Waterhouses (Tel: 0538 308313).

2. Peak National Park Cycle Hire, Waterhouses (Tel: 0538 308609).

Route Instructions:

The trail follows the valley of the River Manifold between Hulme End and Wetton Mill and the valley of the River Hamps between Wetton Mill and Waterhouses. If ever in doubt, follow signs which say No Cars or Motorbikes.

THE CHURNET VALLEY TRAIL

(Between Oakamoor and Denstone, to the west of Ashbourne)

A 4-mile trail through woodland on a dismantled railway at the southwest edge of the Peak District. The ride runs along the bottom of the valley formed by the River Churnet, with steep hills either side. You will probably be aware of music drifting over from Alton Towers Theme Park which lies in the parkland to the north of the valley. Also keep an eye out for the dramatic Gothic-style castle of Alton village to the south of the trail.

Background and places of interest

- **Alton Towers**
More than 125 rides and attractions for a single entrance fee set within 500 acres of gardens and parkland. Open April to October. Tel: 0538 702200.

- **Alton Village**
A fine 14th-century church, a village lock-up used to cool tempers and restrain ruffians and, sitting above the valley, giving the area its nickname of the 'Staffordshire Rhineland', is the Gothic-style castle built by Pugin, the 19th-century architect famous for his work on the House of Commons.

- **Hawksmoor Nature Reserve**
(on the B5417 between Oakamoor and Cheadle)
Woodland trails and industrial archaeology.

- **Froghall Basin, Foxt Road, Froghall**
(3 miles north of Cheadle on the A521)
Terminus of the restored Caldon Canal which carried limestone from nearby quarries to Stoke. Three-hour narrowboat trips available on Thursday mornings and Sunday afternoons. Tel: 0538 266486.

- **Foxfield Steam Railway**
(just off A50 at Blythe Bridge, east of Stoke)
Steam locomotives pull coaches on a 4-mile ride over steep gradients and sharp curves on a line that was once used to transport coal. Museum, souvenir shop, refreshments.

Open Sunday and Bank Holiday Weekends (Saturday, Sunday, Monday) from Easter to September. Tel: 0782 314532 or 396210.

Alton Towers. *AA Picture Library*

Starting Points:
1. The car park near the Admiral Jervis PH in Oakamoor, on the B5417 between Stoke-on-Trent and Ashbourne.
2. The Village Hall, Denstone, on the B5032 5 miles north of Uttoxeter.

Parking:
1. The car park in Oakamoor is just off the B5417, at the bottom of the hill just to the west of the bridge over the River Churnet, by the Admiral Jervis PH. Go to the end of the second car park and fork left to get to the start of the trail.
2. The Village Hall car park, on the B5032 in Denstone, 5 miles north of Uttoxeter. From the car park, go past the petrol station and turn left just before the telephone box on to the Old Churnet Railway trail.

Distance: 4 miles (8 miles round trip).

Map: Ordnance Survey Landranger Sheet 119.

Hills: None.

Surface: In general good. One or two rough patches, with a probability of mud after rain.

Roads and road crossings: None.

Refreshments:
The Tavern PH, Denstone.
The Admiral Jervis PH, Oakamoor

Route Instructions:
(See also 'Parking'.)
As with so many of the routes in this book, the hardest part of the route-finding lies in getting yourself to the start of the ride. Once you have found the start you simply follow the dismantled railway to its end.

Above: *Stockfile*

Right: Alton Towers. *AA Picture Library*

ROUTE 13
Churnet
Valley Trail

B4517

Oakamoor

CHEADLE ←

Admiral Jervis PH

Ⓟ

Alton Park

Alton ● 🏰
castle

B5032

Ⓟ ■
The
Tavern PH
●
Denstone

UTTOXETER
↓

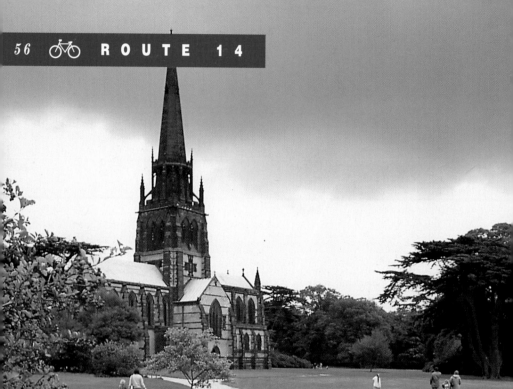

CLUMBER COUNTRY PARK
(Southeast of Worksop)

A 5-mile circuit on tarmac roads around the lake and through the beautiful parkland of Clumber Country Park. There may be a little traffic, but the ride has the advantage of being rideable all year round, whatever the weather. The kitchen garden and the chapel are well worth visiting.

Background and places of interest

• Clumber Park
Over 3,800 acres of parkland and forest, once owned by the Dukes of Newcastle, are now in the care of the National Trust. The house was demolished in 1938, a victim of heavy taxation. Although a new house was planned, the park was requisitioned by the War Department and the new house was never built. Churchill visited the park during the war to watch the trials of the 'White Rabbit', a machine which was able to dig vast trenches with ease.

• The Kitchen Garden Exhibition
Located in the Vineries and Palm House. A splendid range of late 19th-century glasshouses. It includes a collection of gardening implements from the past.

• Hardwick Village
This late 19th-century estate village includes Clumber's Home Farm and cottages built by the 7th Duke of Newcastle for his labourers. Note the steeply pitched roofs and the massive chimney stacks.

• Clumber Lake
Covers 87 acres and took 15 years to build (1774-1789). It is visited by an exceptional variety of wildfowl.

• Clumber Bridge
The beautiful classical bridge spans the narrowest point of the lake, with a superb view towards Clumber Chapel. Built in 1770.

• Clumber Chapel
'A cathedral in miniature'. Lavishly decorated Anglo-Catholic chapel built for the house and estate in 1889 by the 7th Duke of Newcastle.

Open daily April to October 10.00am-5.00pm.

Above: Clumber Chapel. *AA Picture Library*   Right: *Stockfile*

Starting Point: The car park near the site of the old mansion.

Parking: There are five entrances to the park, which lies to the southeast of Worksop. The entrances are off the A57 from the north, off the B6034 to the west and off the A614 to the east. Follow signs.

Distance: 5 miles.

Map: Ordnance Survey Landranger Sheet 120. A very good large-scale map of the park is available for a small charge from the National Trust, Clumber Park Stableyard, Worksop, Nottinghamshire S80 3BE. Tel: 0909 486411.

Hills: Gently undulating.

Surface: Tarmac. One short section of chalk road.

Roads and road crossings: There are some vehicles on the park roads, although there are signs warning motorists that they are likely to come across children on bikes. There is more traffic on Limetree Avenue, the public road that runs northeast between the B6034 near Carburton and the A614 at Appleyard Lodge.

Refreshments: Clumber Restaurant.

Cycle Hire: Available from the building that used to be the Duke's Garage. Open daily 10.00am-4.00pm Easter to September. During winter weekends it is open according to hours of daylight and weather conditions. Tel: 0909 476592.

Route Instructions:

1. From the car park, follow the road alongside the lake. At the crossroads turn left, then left again at the next junction.

2. Cross the bridge and take the road uphill. After 1.5 miles you will eventually come to a Cycle Track Board on your left indicating the white chalk track that links the park roads and avoids having to use the main A614.

3. At the end of a bumpy section, join the tarmac road and follow it downhill to the ford. Go through Hardwick Village and turn left by the war memorial.

4. At the road junction after 0.5 mile, bear left. At the T-junction turn left, then left again at the bus shelter.

5. Go around the cricket pavilion, continuing on the road through the trees. Turn left at the main park road to return to the car park.

THE FIVE PITS TRAIL

(Temple Normanton,
5 miles southeast of Chesterfield)

The Five Pits Trail follows the dismantled railway track that used to serve the collieries. It passes through rolling countryside to the southeast of Chesterfield with fine views, comprising a circuit at the north end around Holmewood and a there-and-back section from south of Williamthorpe to Tibshelf. There are a couple of hills which come as a surprise for anyone expecting a dismantled railway route to be completely flat!

Background and nearby places of interest

The railways used in this ride were opened in 1892 to serve the expanding coalfield and operated initially by the Midland Railway Company's mineral line and later by the Great Central Railway Company. The railway served the five pits of Tibshelf, Pilsley, Holmewood, Williamthorpe and Grassmoor. By 1971 the collieries it served had closed, causing the closure of the railway.

Pilsley coal received royal patronage when Queen Mary (wife of King George V) chose to burn nothing but 'Pilsley Brights' on her drawing room fire at Buckingham Palace.

• Hardwick Hall and Country Park

(3 miles south of Junction 29 of the M1)
An Elizabethan country house built for Bess of Hardwick and now owned by the National Trust. Its spectacular architecture and many windows led to the rhyme 'Hardwick Hall more glass than wall'. Walled courtyards enclose fine gardens, orchards and a herb garden.
Tel: 0246 850430.

• Midland Railway Centre, Butterley Station, Ripley

(6 miles south of Tibshelf)
Passenger trains normally hauled by steam locomotives. Miniature railway and narrow-gauge railway. Brittain Pit Farm Park with many varieties of animals. Tel: 0773 570140.

CHESTERFIELD

START

Grassmoor

B6039

A617

M1
Jct 29

Holmewood

A6175

A6175

Timberlane Picnic Site

ROUTE 15
Five Pits Trail

Tibshelf

Tibshelf Ponds

Picture: Hardwick Hall. *AA Picture Library*

Starting Point: The Birkin Lane car park between Temple Normanton and Grassmoor.

Parking (as above):

1. From Chesterfield. Take the A617 Mansfield road out of Chesterfield for 4 miles. Turn off south on to the B6425, then take the B6039, following signs for Temple Normanton and Holmewood. Turn first right. The car park is 0.75 mile along on your right.

2. From Junction 29 of the M1 take the A6175 towards Clay Cross. At the roundabout in Williamthorpe, turn right on to the B6039, then after 1.25 miles turn first left. The car park is 0.75 mile along this road on your right.

Distance: 6 miles for the circuit and a further 3.5 miles each way to Tibshelf Ponds.

Map: Ordnance Survey Landranger Sheet 120.

Hills: The trail is generally undulating, with a pronounced climb at the start and another just before Tibshelf.

Surface: In general good gravel tracks.

Roads and road crossings: The busy A6175 is crossed twice and the B6039 once.

Refreshments: The Wheatsheaf PH, Tibshelf.

Route Instructions:

1. Follow Five Pits Trail signs from the car park under the bridge and continue up a steady climb. At the fork of tracks, bear left past the pond signposted 'Williamthorpe' (the right fork goes directly to Tibshelf).

2. Cross the B6039. At a crossroads of tracks at a bridge over a stream go straight ahead (the right turn is signposted 'Holmewood wheelchair route').

3. Soon after a new distribution centre, cross the road and continue up a ramp. Follow this road for 100yds then cross the busy A6175, following 'Five Pits Trail' signs.

4. Cross the B6039. After a mile, join the lane by Timberlane picnic site for 50yds.

5. Follow the route through to Tibshelf, dropping down into then climbing out of the valley formed by Westwood Brook. When you are almost level with the church in Tibshelf, fork left under the bridge to go under the road. The route ends at Tibshelf Ponds.

Return

6. Retrace your steps for 3.5 miles as far as the Timberlane picnic site. Less than 0.5 mile after the picnic site, fork left, signposted 'Grassmoor' (the right fork is your outward route via Holmewood).

7. Just before the A6175, with a wooden gate across the obvious path, you will need to turn sharp left downhill in order to cross the main road slightly to the west of this point. Rejoin the outward route to return to the start.

Picture opposite: *Nick Cotton*

THE PLEASLEY TRAILS

(4 miles northwest of Mansfield)

The Pleasley Trails are three separate dismantled railway paths lying between Pleasley, Skegby and Teversal. They are linked together in this ride to form a circular route, passing through some deep cuttings which show the magnesian limestone of the area.

Background and nearby places of interest

The Pleasley Trails network runs along the track beds of the Great Northern Railway and the Midland Railway. The sections explored in this ride were built between 1866 and 1900 and closed between 1965 and 1982.

The Carnarvon Arms at Fackley is named after Lord Carnarvon who, in the 1920s, sponsored Howard Carter's expedition to Egypt which led to the discovery of Tutankhamun's tomb.

The church of St Catherine, Teversal, has a picture-book story of its patron saint's legend carved in 19 symbols around the door.

• Hardwick Hall

(3 miles west of Pleasley)

A well-preserved Elizabethan mansion in a country park, with Elizabethan enclosed garden and rare whiteface woodland sheep and longhorn cattle.

• Bolsover Castle

(5 miles northwest of Pleasley)

The remains of a 17th-century mansion on the site of a Norman castle rise above the countryside on a hilltop. The Little Castle is a folly, a fantasy of pinnacles and turrets.

Starting Point: The car park on Outgang Lane, 0.5 mile east of Pleasley.

Parking: Turn off the A617 Mansfield to Chesterfield road at the roundabout in Pleasley on to the B6407 signposted Shirebrook, then after 200yds turn first right, signposted 'Pleasley Vale & Pleasley Church'. The car park is on the right after 0.75 mile.

Distance: 7 miles.

Map: Ordnance Survey Landranger Sheet 120.

Hills: None.

Surface: Narrow, stone-based trail.

Roads and road crossings: There is a short section on the road in Pleasley near the start of the ride.

Refreshments: Carnarvon Arms PH, between Teversal and Fackley (just off the route).

Route Instructions:

1. Go down from the car park to the stream and turn right, following the stream. Take the underpass beneath the road.

2. Turn right on the road by the Post Office (a bus stop is to your left). Climb the hill, passing the Nag's Head PH on the right.

Picture: Bolsover Castle. *AA Picture Library*

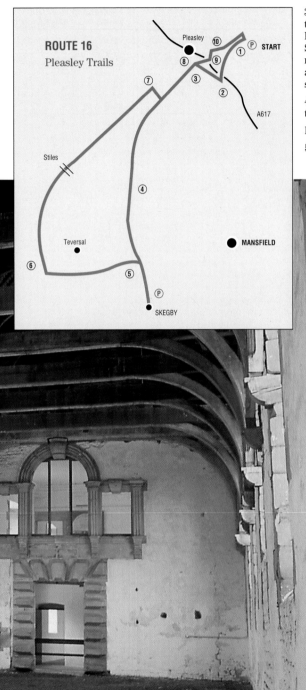

ROUTE 16

Pleasley Trails

Pleasley

START

A617

Stiles

Teversal

MANSFIELD

SKEGBY

3. Just before the roundabout, turn left on to a No Through Road opposite the Pleasley Surgery. Just before a double metal gate, turn left through a wooden barrier to get to the start of the trail.

4. Follow this trail for 2.5 miles to the car park at Skegby.

Return

5. At the fork of tracks, bear left.

6. After a mile, shortly after going under a bridge, where the track appears to end, go straight ahead up some wooden steps, continuing in the same direction. At the road, turn right for 200yds, go under the bridge and immediately right up the steps, then right along the old railway.

7. You will need to lift your bikes over a couple of stiles either side of the road towards Norwood. At a T-junction with a slag heap ahead, turn right for 100yds then left to rejoin the outward route.

8. Join tarmac. At the T-junction with the road near the roundabout, with Pleasley Surgery ahead, turn right then immediately left down an alley signposted 'No Cycling', so get off your bike and push it for 50yds.

9. At the T-junction at the end of Booth Lane, turn left then cross the dual carriageway via the footbridge.

10. Go past the church. At the end of Church Lane, turn right for 400yds to return to the car park at the start.

CLIPSTONE FOREST, SHERWOOD

(Northeast of Mansfield)

A well-signposted trail through this large tract of forestry land. The tracks are wide and well-maintained and the route is waymarked with red-painted wooden markers, so no instructions are needed. The width of the trail means this is a good ride for cycling in a group and having a chat! There is an adjoining, tougher mountain bike trail if you want to try something more adventurous.

This is the only Forestry Commission ride described in detail; for more Forestry Commission routes, see page 102.

Background and nearby places of interest

• **Clipstone Forest**

This forms part of one of the largest single tracts of woodland in the East Midlands. Most of the forest was planted in the 1920s and 1930s in the early days of the Forestry Commission. The age of the tree crop means that large areas have been harvested and replanted in recent years. Much of the timber produced here has supplied local businesses, particularly as pit wood for the mining

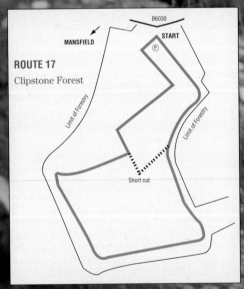

Picture. Clipstone Forest. *Nick Cotton*

industry. In some parts of the forest the heathland vegetation, once so common in Sherwood, still exists. These areas are now being kept as heathland as part of the conservation plan.

● **The Sherwood Forest Country Park, north of Edwinstowe**

The oak and birch woodland with open grassland and heath has probably changed little since Robin Hood was said to have lived in the forest. The Visitor Centre provides toilets, refreshments and a Robin Hood exhibition.

Legend says that Robin Hood and Maid Marian were married in nearby Edwinstowe church.

Tel: 0623 823202.

● **The Sherwood Forest Farm Park, Lamb Pens Farm, Edwinstowe**
(midway between Edwinstowe and Mansfield Woodhouse, just off the A6075)

A large display of rare and interesting breeds of cattle, sheep, pigs, goats and wildfowl.

Open daily April to mid-October.
Tel: 0623 823558.

● **The ruins of King John's Palace**

These lie in the fields close to the Dog & Duck PH near Old Clipstone, to the north of the forest. The palace was built as a royal hunting centre for the Royal Forest of Sherwood, but by the 17th century the forest had been split up and the palace fell into disrepair.

Starting Point: Sherwood Pines car park, off the B6030, 5 miles northeast of Mansfield.

Parking: As above.

Distance: 6-mile circuit.

Map: Ordnance Survey Landranger Sheet 120. Map also available from Forestry Commission, Forest Enterprise, Sherwood and Lincs Forest District, Edwinstowe, Mansfield, Notts NG21 9JL. Tel: 0623 822447.

Hills: Undulating, but no hill involves more than 100ft of climbing.

Surface: Forestry track quality, with occasional short, muddy sections.

Roads and road crossings: None.

Refreshments: Cafe open near the Information Centre, 10.00am-3.30pm during the week and 10.00am-5.00pm at the weekends (longer hours in the summer, shorter in the winter).

Route Instructions:
If you make your way from the car park towards the Information Centre you will come across the red markers that indicate the route of the trail.

Above: Sherwood Forest Country Park Visitors' Centre.
AA Picture Library

Main Picture: Clipstone Forest. *Nick Cotton*

SHIPLEY COUNTRY PARK
(West of Nottingham)

An attractive and interesting circular ride in this country park. A curious juxtaposition of old mining equipment, woodland, lakes and even views into an American Theme Park. The tracks are well-signposted and in general well-maintained. This ride is one of many loops that could be made within the park on tracks or lanes with little traffic.

Background and places of interest

• Shipley Park

A medieval estate, mentioned in the Domesday Book, Shipley was developed during the 18th century as a farming and coal-mining area by the influential Miller Mundy family. Fine lodges and cottages dating from this period can still be seen around the park. Following restoration of the old coal mine sites, former railway lines have become walkways and cyclepaths, and reclaimed colliery spoils are now woodland and wildflower meadows.

• American Adventure

Adjacent to the country park is a Theme Park, under separate management. Tel: 0773 769931.

Starting Point: The car park/Information Centre at the entrance to Shipley Park, 1 mile south of Heanor, 8 miles west of Nottingham.

Parking: As above. Signposted from the A608 Heanor to Derby road and the A6007 Heanor to Ilkeston road.

Distance: 6.5 miles.

Map: Ordnance Survey Landranger Sheet 129.

Hills: One fairly steep 150-ft climb to the hill in the centre of the park.

Surface: Varies from tarmac lane to good stone track. Occasional short muddy sections.

Roads and road crossings: There is a small lane with occasional traffic running north from Mapperley to Heanor which is used for a short section near Mapperley.

Refreshments:
Cafe at the Information Centre open seven days a week from 11.00am-5.00pm, April to the end of October. From November to the end of March at weekends only. Black Horse PH at Mapperley.

Cycle Hire: June to early September, seven days a week 9.30am-5.00pm. During the rest of the year at weekends only. Tel: 0773 719961.

Route Instructions:
1. From the car park near the Information Centre, follow signs for Osborne's Pond (marked with blue horseshoes). Stay on the track in the wood by the pond, then follow a small lane to your right.

2. At the end of the metal railings on your right, turn right down a tarmac track signposted 'Shipley Hill'.

3. At the top of a steep hill, turn sharp left past a lodge, signposted 'Shipley Wood'. There are fine views into the American Theme Park.

4. At the bottom of the hill, cross the bridge over the lake then turn immediately right on to a tarmac lane. Follow this lane as it turns sharp right then sharp left by the farm.

5. Follow signs for Mapperley then take the first right, signposted 'Mapperley Reservoir'.

OR, if you wish to visit the pub in Mapperley, carry on straight ahead. At the crossroads in Mapperley at the end of Coronation Road, turn right on to the No Through Road signposted

'Bridleway to Heanor'. Go past the lake on your left.

6. (Main route) Join the tarmac road at the lake. Turn right then just past the car park on the left, take the SECOND gravel track on the left by a wide wooden gate. Follow the main track (the reservoir is to your left) through woodland. At a T-junction with a better tarmac track, turn right then second left, following signs for the Visitors Centre.

Pictures on this page: *Stockfile*

FROM ELVASTON COUNTRY PARK ALONG THE RIVER DERWENT TO DERBY

This ride links the very heart of Derby with the delightful parkland of Elvaston Castle and Country Park via a well-maintained track alongside the River Derwent. You have the impression of sneaking into Derby via a secret passage, so well segregated is the route from the busy roads into the city. Along the riverside track is a real bike playground — with ramps and bumps — where you can hone your cycling-trick skills.

Background and places of interest

• Elvaston Castle

The imposing stone and brick-built house dates from the early 19th century. Only open for special events and exhibitions, the house is situated in 200 acres of beautiful wood and parkland containing many rare trees planted over 150 years ago. There is an adventure playground, an ornamental garden, a topiary, an Old English garden with herbaceous borders and a rose garden. The gardens are free and open all year round.

• The Estate Museum, Elvaston Castle

Recreates life on the Elvaston Castle Estate around 1910. Original workshops and cottages show the life and work of the craftsmen, tradesmen and labourers.

Open Easter to end-October.

• Bike Playground

About 2 miles after joining the riverside path, shortly after going underneath a wide road bridge, you will come across a park with prepared hills, bumps and ramps for practising tricks and stunts!

• Castle Donington

(6 miles southeast of Elvaston)
Aeropark and Visitors Centre, East Midlands Airport. History of aviation with cut-away models of aircraft cabins.

Open seven days a week April to October, weekends only November to March. Tel: 0332 810621.

• The Donington Collection

(on A453 next to motor racing circuit)
This has the world's largest collection of single-seater racing cars. Videos of the history of motor racing. Tel: 0332 810048.

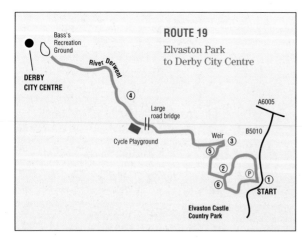

ROUTE 19
Elvaston Park to Derby City Centre

Starting Points:
1. Car park in Elvaston Country Park.
2. Bass's Recreation Ground, between the bus and railway stations in the centre of Derby.

Parking: (For Elvaston Park) Take the A6005 out of Derby towards Long Eaton. In Borrowash, turn off on to the B5010. The entrance to the park is about 1.25 miles along on the right.

Distance: Circuit of Elvaston Country Park — 2 miles. From the park to the centre of Derby — 4.5 miles (9 miles round trip).

Map: Ordnance Survey Landranger Sheets 128 and 129.

Hills: None.

Surface: Good gravel track.

Roads and road crossings: None (unless you start in Derby and have to make your way to the Council Hall).

Refreshments: The Parlour Tea Rooms at Elvaston Castle, open daily from Easter to the end of October.

Route Instructions:
(from Elvaston into Derby)

1. From the car park off the B5010, go back towards the road and take the track on the left just inside the park boundary. Follow this as far as the castle. At the castle turn right on to tarmac (or left to visit the castle).

2. Just after a sharp left-hand bend, use the raised pavement running to the left of the tarmac lane. Where you rejoin the tarmac lane, go straight ahead on to the track past the fir tree. (Or turn left for a circuit of Elvaston Park.) After 400yds, turn first right by a litter bin through a wooden bridle gate.

3. Join the river near a weir, and turn left.

4. Follow this riverside track for 4.5 miles as far as Bass's Recreation Ground. If you wish to continue as far as the Council House, you will need to dismount.

From Bass's Recreation Ground, Derby city centre to Elvaston

5. Follow the riverside path from the corner of the park for 4.5 miles. Turn off from the riverside path at the weir, where the pylons cross to the other side of the river.

6. At a T-junction after 0.5 mile, turn left. At the T-junction at the large fir tree, turn right to complete a circuit of the park.

Picture: *Stockfile*

THE STAFFORD NEWPORT GREENWAY
(West of Stafford)

A short ride along a stretch of dismantled railway near Stafford. Probably at its best in late spring and summer when there are wildflowers and butterflies to be seen. Why not take a wildflower book with you? Do not pick the flowers, however; leave them for others to see.

Background and places of interest

The line was built in 1849 by the Shropshire Union Railway and ran from Stafford to Newport and Wellington and beyond, being an important link between the Midlands and Wales. The line was used for 115 years until 1964 when the last steam engine plied its way along the line carrying a wreath to mourn its passing. It was replaced by the new more efficient diesel, whose reign, however, was short-lived as the line closed a few months later.

The sides of railway lines, often covered with brambles, hawthorn and rosebay willowherb, have always been habitats for wildlife, and with the greater variety of trees and plants since the closure of the line, the wildlife has increased. The area is one of the best in Staffordshire for butterfly sightings.

• Stafford
The Ancient High House, built in 1595, is one of the oldest timber-framed town houses in England. Stafford Castle was built on the site of an 11th-century timber Norman castle.

• Shugborough Estate
(4 miles east of Stafford)
The ancestral home of Lord Lichfield, set in 900 acres of beautiful gardens and parkland with an 18th-century mansion house, original servants' quarters and a Georgian farmstead.

Picture: *Nick Cotton*

Starting Points:

1. The new housing estate at Castlefields, 0.5 mile out of Stafford on the A518 Newport road.

2. The car park 0.5 mile north of Haughton, also off the A518 towards Newport from Stafford.

3. The Red Lion PH, Derrington.

Parking:

1. Some parking near the newly built housing estate at Castlefields.

2. Just before the Shropshire Inn PH in Haughton, turn right on to Station Road signposted Ranton 2.5, Eccleshall 6.5. After 0.5 mile, just past Station House, turn left into a small car park.

3. The Red Lion PH, Derrington, off the A518 Stafford to Newport road.

Distance: 3.5 miles (7 miles round trip).

Map: Ordnance Survey Landranger Sheet 127.

Hills: None.

Surface: Narrow, stone-based track.

Roads and road crossings: None (unless you cycle out from the centre of Stafford).

Refreshments:

Red Lion PH at Derrington (the pub car park backs on to the cycle track)

The Shropshire Inn PH at Haughton.

Route Instructions:

1. To get to the start of the trail from Castlefields (off the A518 towards Newport on the outskirts of Stafford), go straight ahead at the roundabout by the housing estate, then immediately right through wooden gates and left on to a track.

2. Shortly after the factory on your right, turn right on to the course of the old railway.

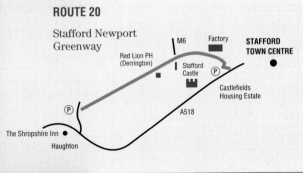

ROUTE 20

Stafford Newport Greenway

TWO ROUTES THROUGH LEICESTER

The route following the River Soar north to the Watermead Park (21) combined with the one going south from St Margaret's Pasture car park (22), forms an almost continuous traffic-free ride from the northern outskirts of Leicester, through the city centre and out into the country on the southern side, almost all through attractive or interesting surroundings. Collectively the area is known as the Riverside Park.

NB. Please see the 'Waterways Code for Cyclists' on page 107.

Background and places of interest

Leicester is proud of its claim as Britain's first Environment City and much has been achieved for cyclists visiting or living in the city. A good degree of this progress has occurred as a result of the efforts of SPOKES, a cycle pressure group who have charted out safe routes for commuters and leisure cyclists alike. They also organise rides for all abilities and ages. They can be contacted at PO Box 30, Leicester LE1 7GD.

• Abbey Park
Includes a boating lake, aviary, extensive pets' corner, miniature railway, children's play area with paddling pool and also the reconstructed site of Leicester Abbey.

• Museum of Technology
(Corporation Road, off Abbey Lane)
The ride goes right past this museum, housed in the Abbey Pumping Station, and formerly part of the city's sewerage system. Original steam beam engines and a transport collection.

• Other Leicester Museums
Leicestershire Museum and Art Gallery (art, ceramics, Egyptology); the Guildhall (14th- to 16th-century Hall, Old Town Library, 19th-century police cells); Jewry Wall Museum (archaeology, local history to 1500, Roman bath site); Newarke House Museum (16th- to 20th-century local history, 19th-century street scene, period garden); Wygston's House (late medieval house, costumes).

Route 21

Starting Point: The St Margaret's Pasture car park near the Sports Centre, just off St Margaret's Way (near Abbey Park in the centre of Leicester).

Parking: As above.

Distance: 3.5 miles (7 miles round trip).

Map: Ordnance Survey Landranger Sheet 140. A very useful booklet for the area is called *Cyclists' Leicester: Leicester Spokes Street by Street Guide to Environment City*, available for £2.95 from Leicester Spokes, PO Box 30, Leicester LE1 7GD.

Hills: None.

Surface: Good-quality all-year-round tracks, much of them tarmac. The furthest stretch, near the White Horse PH in Birstall, may be a little muddy.

Roads and road crossings: The roads are crossed via pelican crossings.

Refreshments:
White Horse PH and the Plough PH, Birstall, next to Watermead Park.

Refreshments are also available in Abbey Park and at the Gazebo Cafe in the Abbey Grounds, opposite the old stone bridge into the park.

Route Instructions:
1. At the end of the car park, turn left between the black iron railings, with the sports centre on your left. (Or you may wish to go straight ahead into Abbey Park for a tour around the lake.)

2. Continue halfway around the sports ground then turn right over the concrete river bridge. At the end of the bridge, turn right again, signposted 'Riverside Way/Birstall'. You will follow blue-and-white markers for the majority of the way.

3. At a T-junction, just after the Museum of Technology on your left, turn right and follow the river (do not cross the steel bridge). Remember this point for your return so as not to miss the turning.

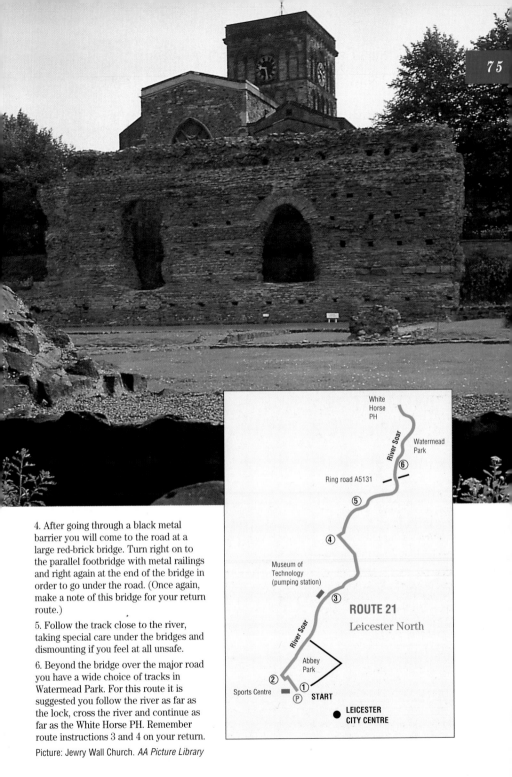

4. After going through a black metal barrier you will come to the road at a large red-brick bridge. Turn right on to the parallel footbridge with metal railings and right again at the end of the bridge in order to go under the road. (Once again, make a note of this bridge for your return route.)

5. Follow the track close to the river, taking special care under the bridges and dismounting if you feel at all unsafe.

6. Beyond the bridge over the major road you have a wide choice of tracks in Watermead Park. For this route it is suggested you follow the river as far as the lock, cross the river and continue as far as the White Horse PH. Remember route instructions 3 and 4 on your return.

Picture: Jewry Wall Church. *AA Picture Library*

White Horse PH

River Soar

Watermead Park

⑥

Ring road A5131

⑤

④

Museum of Technology (pumping station)

③

ROUTE 21
Leicester North

River Soar

Abbey Park

②   ①
Sports Centre   ℗   **START**

● **LEICESTER CITY CENTRE**

ROUTE 22

Leicester South

Route 22

From the centre of Leicester south to Blaby and on to the Grand Union Canal. This route heads south along the Great Central Way that follows the course of a dismantled railway, then drops down on to the towpath of the Grand Union Canal as far as a picnic site by Crow Mill. NB. Please see the 'Waterways Code for Cyclists' on page 107.

Starting Point: The St Margaret's Pasture car park in the centre of Leicester, near the Sports Centre just off St Margaret's Way (near Abbey Park in the city centre).

Parking: As above.

Distance: 7.5 miles (15 miles round trip).

Map: Ordnance Survey Landranger Sheet 140. See also details of *Cyclists' Leicester* in route 21.

Hills: None.

Surface: The first half of the ride is all on tarmac. The second half is on good-quality towpath.

Roads and road crossings: Roads are crossed via special cycle crossings.

Refreshments: Some choice in and near Abbey Park at the start. The County Arms PH in Blaby, just by the canal.

Tips and warnings: Sections of this ride go alongside canals. Dismount to go under the low bridges, ride slowly and let people know you are coming, with a bell or a 'Hello'. To get your bike through the barriers, tip it on to its back wheel, pull the bike's handlebars up to chest height and 'walk' the bike through narrow gaps.

Route Instructions:

1. From the car park, go back to the main road and turn left down the steps on to the towpath. At the towpath turn right under the bridge.

2. Shortly after passing North Bridge (there is a lock here), fork left then soon leave the canal towpath at the next bridge (made of metal,

Picture: Urban cycling, Leicester. *Stockfile*

painted red), bearing right to cross the bridge. Shortly, turn left on to Forest Way.

3. At the traffic lights at the main road at the end of Richard III Road, use the special cyclists' traffic lights to cross the main road and go on to the pavement on the left-hand side of the road opposite. Follow the pavement for 50yds, then use the red-and-green stepped metal ramp to climb on to the Great Central Way.

4. Follow the cycle track for 3 miles until the end of the tarmac. Shortly after the end of the tarmac, which comes 800yds after a large underpass and 300yds past a sign for Blaby, turn right by a metal gate and a wooden post signposted Blue Bank Lock.

5. Follow the obvious track to the canal towpath, lift your bike over the left-hand stile, descend to the towpath and continue for 3 miles to bridge number 92 at Crow Mill, by the totem pole. Beyond this point the surface of the towpath soon deteriorates, so it is suggested that you turn around at this point.

Return:

A. On your way back keep your eye out for Blue Bank Lock; exit here to rejoin the Great Central Way back into Leicester.

B. Descend the ramp at the end of the cycle path. Stay on the right-hand pavement and get into the designated cyclists' lane at the traffic lights to cross the main road on to Richard III Road.

C. At a tall black metal signpost turn right over a red metal bridge to cross the river then bear left down on to the canal towpath just before the second bridge.

D. Go up the steps by Abbey Road Bridge, past the toilets into the car park at the start.

Main Picture: Jewry Wall Church.
Inset: Clock Tower.
AA Picture Library

RUTLAND WATER
(12 miles east of Leicester)

The largest man-made lake in Western Europe, covering an area of 3,100 acres. It is one of the best and most well-organised cycling attractions in the country, with cycle hire, plenty to see and do, a well-signposted circular route around the edge of the reservoir and lots of refreshment stops.

ROUTE 23
Rutland Water

OAKHAM ←

Barnsdale (P)
Whitwell
Empingham (P)
(P)
A1 →

Egleton •
Hambleton Peninsula

(P) Normanton

Manton •
Edith Weston •

LEICESTER ↘
Road section: extra care

Background and places of interest

- **Butterfly and Aquatic Centre, Empingham Leisure Area**
Tropical butterflies and plants, exotic insects and fish in unique surroundings.

- **Adventure Playground, Empingham Leisure Area**

- **Normanton Church and Water Museum, Normanton Leisure Area**
The museum houses a display portraying the local history of the area now covered by Rutland Water, over a 200 million year timespan. Documents and photographs describe the last two centuries' local history, with a detailed display and video of the reservoir's construction during the 1970s. The museum is open every day from 1 April to 30 October and at weekends until 15 December.

- **Drought Garden, Barnsdale Leisure Area**
Created by Anglian Water to demonstrate the wide variety of attractive plants and shrubs which can be grown successfully in the British climate and which require no extra watering. The arboretum, next to the drought garden, is planted with all the tree species, other than willows, used in Anglian Water's extensive planting programme. Twenty-one species grow in a spinney along a clearly signed route.

Picture: *Nick Cotton*

Starting Points: There are four main car parks around the lake — one on the southern side at Normanton and three on the north side at Barnsdale, Whitwell and Empingham (Sykes Lane) Park Areas. All the car parks are some 6 miles west of Stamford (on the A1) and 5 miles east of Oakham (on the A606 and A6003).

Parking: As above.

Distance: The circuit of the lake is some 17 miles. The trip around the Upper Hambleton peninsula is a further 6 miles. The best sections are around the eastern half of the lake.

Map: Ordnance Survey Landranger Sheet 141.

Hills: Although the cycle route runs around the edge of a lake, there are one or two hills, notably near the Barnsdale Park Area and on the peninsula.

Surface: Good all-year-round track, at times tarmac.

Roads and road crossings: There is a section along the lane which leads from the A606 near Oakham on to the peninsula, but it is fairly quiet. Similarly, the lane to Egleton is quiet. There is, however, a busier section of just over a

mile on the road leading from Manton to Normanton, where extra care should be taken.

Refreshments:
Anti-clockwise from Normanton:
The Wheatsheaf PH, Edith Weston

The Fox and Hounds PH, Exton

The White Horse PH, Empingham. Coffee, lunches and afternoon teas

Noel Arms PH, Whitwell. Also open for morning coffee and afternoon teas

The Finch's Arms PH, Hambleton

Horse and Jockey PH, Manton

Cycle Hire:
1. Whitwell: April-October daily 9.15am-7.00pm. February, March and November daily 9.30am-5.30pm. December/January weekends 9.30am to dusk. Tel 0780 86705.

2. Normanton: March to end-October. Weekends and school holidays. Tel: 0780 720888.

Route Instructions:
The route is in general well signposted. If you do not want to go on to the peninsula, follow signs for Egleton and avoid Hambleton.

Picture: Sculpture, Rutland Water. *AA Picture Library*

THE BRAMPTON VALLEY WAY
(Between Northampton and Market Harborough)

The longest dismantled railway cycle trail in the southern Midlands. A good-quality surface track connecting Market Harborough with the northern outskirts of Northampton. There is plenty to see and do and lots of places to visit close to the trail, although most, unfortunately, involve climbing out of the valley. There are some old steam locomotives and rolling stock at Chapel Brampton. You will have to go through at least one tunnel so it is as well to have a torch or bike lights with you.

Background and places of interest

The railway line was closed in 1981 and purchased by Northamptonshire County Council in 1987. It opened for recreational use as the Brampton Valley Way in 1993. It is named after the tributary of the River Nene — the Brampton Arm, the valley of which it follows for much of its length.

- **Harborough Museum**
  (Adam and Eve Street, Market Harborough)
  Illustrating the medieval planned town and its role as a market place, a social and hunting centre and a stagecoach post.
  Open Monday to Saturday 10.00am-4.30pm, Sunday 2.00-5.00pm. Admission free.

- **Brixworth Country Park**
  (1 mile off the route)
  An idyllic place for a picnic with glorious views of the surrounding countryside and Pitsford Water.

- **Althorp House, Althorp**
  (4 miles west of the Northampton end of the route)
  The family home of the Princess of Wales is filled with one of the finest art collections in the world.

- **Foxton Locks**
  (3 miles northwest of Market Harborough)
  Landscaped car park and picnic site with a woodland footpath to Grand Union Canal towpath, a long flight of locks and remains of a barge lift on an inclined plane.

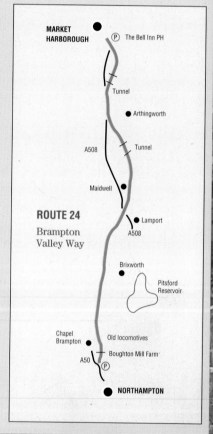

ROUTE 24
Brampton Valley Way

Brampton Valley Way. *Nick Cotton*

Surface: Broad, good-quality stone-based track along the whole length.

Roads and road crossings: One crossing needing care — the A508 Market Harborough to Northampton road.

Refreshments: Three picnic sites adjacent to the car parks. Lots of pubs within a mile of the route:

George Inn PH, Red Lion PH, Coach and Horses PH, Brixworth (this involves a steep climb on road away from the railway path)

Stags Head PH, Maidswell

Bulls Head PH, Arthingworth

Spencer Arms Tavern, village store, Chapel Brampton

Starting Points:

1. The Bell Inn PH car park, Market Harborough.

2. Brampton Valley Way car park, Boughton Crossing, Northampton.

Parking:

1. From the traffic lights in the centre of Market Harborough, follow the A508 Northampton road for 0.5 mile. The Bell Inn PH is on your left. The cycle path starts at the back of the pub.

2. From the centre of Northampton, follow the A50 towards Leicester for 4 miles. Once out beyond the town limits and into the country, take the first right (Brampton Lane) signposted 'Boughton 1¼, Moulton 3, Boughton Cold Store', then immediately turn right again into the car park.

Distance: 14 miles (28 miles round trip).

Maps: Ordnance Survey Landranger Sheets 141 and 152.

Hills: None (unless you have to avoid the tunnels).

The old Pitsford and Brampton station open for teas on Sundays and Bank Holidays

The George PH, Great Oxendon

The Lamport Swan PH, Lamport

The Cherry Tree PH, Little Bowden

Route Instructions:

A. From the Bell Inn, Market Harborough, turn right on to the railway path and continue as far as you feel you can manage.

B. From the car park off the A50 near Northampton, return to the main road, turn right and stay on the pavement for 100yds then turn right again on to the start of the cycle path.

Pictures (top): Old grammar school, Market Harborough. *AA Picture Library*
(middle): Brampton Valley Way. *Nick Cotton*

THE KINGSWINFORD RAILWAY TRAIL

(From Wombourne, south of Wolverhampton)

Despite its proximity to the conurbation of Wolverhampton, this ride along the disused railway of the Kingswinford line has a very fine, wooded, countryside feel to it. The trail is well-maintained with the exception of its extreme southern end near Pensnett, which is somewhat neglected. Otherwise it is apparent that real pride is taken in keeping the trail in top condition. Along its whole length, the trail runs parallel with the Staffordshire and Worcestershire Canal; indeed, there is an option of extending your ride northwards by following the canal towpath for a few miles before turning round. If you do this extension you are aware how close you are to the hub of the country's canal network, with one canal to the right signposted Birmingham and another to the left signposted Chester.

NB. Please see the 'Waterways Code for Cyclists' on page 107.

Background and places of interest

The railway was built by the Great Western Railway Company as the Kingswinford Branch Railway (a branch off the Worcester to Wolverhampton main line). It was single track except for a few passing loops. The intention was to serve the area to the west of Wolverhampton and Dudley. The line was opened in 1925 but it was not very successful and had only a relatively short working life. Passenger services stopped in 1932 and Wombourne Station was closed in 1966.

The name Wombourne comes from the Old English 'Womburnan', meaning 'winding stream'. The Wom Brook, which runs through the centre of the village, powered several mills along its length.

The Visitor Centre at the Old Station,

Wombourne, is open 12.00-5.00pm at the weekends and Bank Holidays.

• Himley Station

This was built for the convenience of the Earl of Dudley and his guests travelling to Himley Hall. A horse dock was provided at the station for the loading and unloading of horses and his lordship's laundry basket frequently travelled between Himley Hall and his London home in Chelsea! The setting was very rural, rail traffic was very light and the local hunt had precedence over the railway. Pheasants from Himley Plantation frequently wandered round the station.

• The Staffordshire and Worcestershire Canal

Runs for 46 miles from Great Haywood near Stafford to Stourport on the River Severn. One of the original Brindley canals, it opened in 1772 and was one of the main routes to the north from Birmingham before the Shropshire Union Canal was built.

• Red Sandstone Cuttings

You pass through exposed 'cliffs' of red sandstone which are Triassic deposits, formed over 200 million years ago when desert conditions covered the whole area.

Picture: *Stockfile*

Starting Points:

1. The car park at the Old Station at Wombourne.

2. The car park at Himley, south of Wombourne.

3. The car park at Tettenhall, north of Wombourne.

Parking:

1. (Wombourne) Turn off the A449 Wolverhampton to Kidderminster road at the roundabout near Wombourne where the A463 joins the A449, signposted 'Kingswinford Railway Walk/Trysull/Seisdon'. Follow signs for Trysull on to Billy Buns Lane, then just before a brown-and-cream coloured railway bridge, opposite Station Road, turn right on to a track signposted 'Kingswinford Railway Walk/Ye Olde Station Tea Shoppe'.

2. (Himley) Turn off the A449 Wolverhampton to Kidderminster road on to the B4176, signposted 'Bridgnorth'. After 0.75 mile turn first left at Sandiacre Farm Shop on to Himley Lane, signposted 'Halfpenny Green/Swindon'. Go under the bridge and turn first right opposite Long Meadow Boarding Kennels.

Picture: *Nick Cotton*

3. (Tettenhall) Take the A41 from Wolverhampton towards Newport, then at the traffic lights with the B4161, by a petrol station, turn left on to Henwood Road, signposted 'Wightwick Manor/Compton/Bridgnorth/RFU Castlecroft', then turn first left on to Meadow View and first right through gates.

Distance (from Wombourne): 9 miles to the north (6 miles on the railway path, 3 miles on the canal towpath); 3.5 miles to the south.

Map: Ordnance Survey Landranger Sheet 139.

Hills: None.

Surface: Good all-year-round track. (If you go as far south as Pensnett and beyond there is glass and rubbish on the track.)

Roads and road crossings: None.

Refreshments:

Excellent tea shop at the start/finish at Wombourne Station.

Several picnic sites at intervals along the trail.

Greyhound PH, Lower Penn, just off the route at bridge 39 (by a red brickdust 'layby' on the trail between Wombourne and Castlecroft.

Route Instructions:

A. North from Wombourne

1. From the Wombourne car park turn right on to the cycle track. Continue for 3 miles to Castlecroft and a further 3 miles to Aldersley Stadium. Just before going past Tettenhall Station you will cross the Staffordshire and Worcestershire Canal via a large metal bridge. If you choose to do part of the return journey along the canal towpath, you will rejoin the outward route at this point.

2. On arriving at Aldersley Stadium you can either turn round and go back the way you have come or follow the canal towpath for a while. Joining the canal towpath gives you two options: you may go on further and make a longer trip, or you may return to the start a different way.

3. To get to the canal, go downhill towards then past the stadium, leaving it to your left, then go under the railway bridge. At the road, turn left down a track and follow this to a bridge over the canal. At this point you can:

a. for a longer ride, turn left along the canal. The towpath surface is good for about 3 miles north to Brinsford Bridge under the A449. Ignore a canal to the right signposted Birmingham and a second canal, this time to the left and signposted Chester. Shortly after passing the canal to the left, a better, parallel track runs 10yds to the left of the towpath alongside a housing estate.

b. for the shorter ride, with a slightly different return trip, using a short section of the canal towpath, turn right alongside the canal for about 1.25 miles. At the large metal bridge over the river, leave the canal and rejoin the railway track.

B. South from Wombourne

The railway path can be followed for 3.5 miles south — on good surface through woodland — as far as a large chimney at the edge of a waste disposal site. Beyond here the cycle path is not so well maintained and you may come across glass and rubbish.

THE WORCESTER AND BIRMINGHAM CANAL
(Near Tardebigge Locks)

How did the canal builders of the 18th century overcome the problem of hills that could not be avoided? This ride alongside the flight of locks at Tardebigge gives you an opportunity to see how boats can go uphill! The ride starts where the canal disappears into a tunnel beneath the A448. From late spring to early autumn you will see narrowboats slowly making their way up and down this stretch of water.

NB. Please see the 'Waterways Code for Cyclists' on page 107.

Background and places of interest

The Worcester and Birmingham Canal was built 200 years ago and has 58 locks. These start just south of Tardebigge and drop the canal 425ft to the River Severn at Worcester. Lock 58, the deepest narrow lock on the canal, is the start of the 30 locks in the Tardebigge Flight, which is the longest navigable lock flight in the country.

- **Avoncroft Museum of Buildings**
  (3 miles southwest of Bromsgrove)
  A collection of historic buildings spanning seven centuries of English history — from a working windmill and chain-making shop to a 1946 prefab — which have been dismantled and rebuilt here. There are also displays of carts and caravans.

- **Droitwich**
  (southwest of Bromsgrove)
  Visitors to the spa baths can float in buoyant brine pumped up from a lake over a bed of rock salt deposited 200ft under the town.
  The Heritage Centre tells the story of the salt industry.

- **The Forge Mill, Redditch**
  The National Needle Museum is housed in an 18th-century watermill where needles were cleaned and sharpened. The original machinery is still intact and working.

Picture: *Nick Cotton*

ROUTE 26
The Tardebigge Locks on the Worcester and Birmingham Canal

Starting Point: Tardebigge Boat Yard off the B4184 between Bromsgrove and Redditch.

Parking: As above.

Distance: 5 miles (10 miles round trip).

Map: Ordnance Survey Landranger Sheets 150 and 139.

Hills: Surprisingly, for a canal towpath, there is a steady climb from the furthest point back to the start of some 250ft.

Surface: This section of the towpath is in reasonably good condition. Beyond Stoke Wharf it deteriorates, becoming rutted and narrow.

Roads and road crossings: None of any significance.

Refreshments:
Queen's Head PH at Stoke Pound (big garden with swings and slide)

Jan's Kitchen in the Stoke Wharf boatyard does a fine bacon sandwich! (Open Monday-Friday 9.00am-5.00pm and Saturday 9.00am-2.00pm)

Boat and Railway PH, beyond Stoke Works

Route Instructions:
1. From the car park at Tardebigge Boat Yard, turn right uphill. Stay on the pavement and take the first right after the bridge.

2. The towpath is in reasonable condition for 5 miles, as far as the attractive lock-keeper's cottage at lock 18 and bridge 40 (Astwood Bottom Lock). Beyond this point the surface becomes poor. Bear in mind that it will take a lot longer to return to the start than it took on the outward leg as you will be going uphill on the way back.

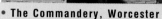

NORTH FROM WORCESTER ALONG THE WORCESTER AND BIRMINGHAM CANAL

For somewhere so full of busy main roads, Worcester nevertheless boasts two very enjoyable traffic-free routes for cycling, both using the banks of waterways. This one runs along the towpath of the Worcester to Birmingham canal, starting where it joins the Severn and heading north for 2.5 miles. The other follows the Severn itself through the town. There is always plenty going on in the Diglis Basin, where the canal joins the river.

NB. Please see the 'Waterways Code for Cyclists' on page 107.

Background and places of interest

• Worcester and Birmingham Canal

Built between 1792 and 1815, the canal is 30 miles long and has 58 locks and five tunnels. Cargoes consisted of coal and industrial goods down to Worcester, whilst grain, building materials and farm produce made the return journey.

Starting Point: Diglis Basin on Diglis Road near the Anchor PH and the junction of the Worcester Canal with the River Severn.

Parking: Follow signs for the A38 (Tewkesbury) out of the centre of Worcester. At Bristol Street Motors and the Albion PH, fork right, signposted Diglis Trading Estate. After 200yds, just past the Anchor PH, you can park on the left. Return with your bikes to the boatyard.

Distance: 2.5 miles (5 miles round trip).

Map: Ordnance Survey Landranger Sheet 150. *The Nicholson and Ordnance Survey Guide to the Waterways (South)* covers all the canals in southern England and the southern part of the Midlands.

Hills: None.

Picture: Worcester. *AA Picture Library*

• The Commandery, Worcester

It was in this magnificent 15th-century timber-framed building that Charles II planned his campaign during the Battle of Worcester in 1651, the last major conflict of the Civil War. The displays in the Great Hall use a wide-screen multi-projector to give you an idea of life during the Civil War.

Open daily all year. Tel: 0905 355071.

• Worcester Cathedral

One of England's finest cathedrals, it has dominated the city for 900 years. Famous for its music, it is one of the homes of the Three Choirs, Europe's oldest music festival. Features include Edgar Tower, the Norman chapter house, the medieval cloisters and the tomb of King John. From the cathedral gardens there are views over the Severn to the Malvern Hills.

• The Guildhall

This has one of the finest baroque façades in existence. Inside are heritage displays.

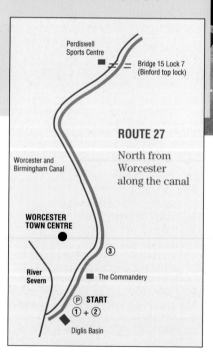

Perdiswell Sports Centre

Bridge 15 Lock 7 (Binford top lock)

Worcester and Birmingham Canal

ROUTE 27

North from Worcester along the canal

WORCESTER TOWN CENTRE

③

River Severn

■ The Commandery

Ⓟ **START**
① + ②

Diglis Basin

Surface: The towpath is well maintained as far as the sports centre at Perdiswell.

Roads and road crossings: None.

Refreshments:
The Canalside Tearooms next to the Commandery, Worcester.

Lots of choice in Worcester.

Route Instructions:
1. To reach the junction of the Worcester and Birmingham Canal with the River Severn, pass to the left of Worcester Yacht Chandlers (a brick building painted white) from the entrance to the boatyard. Cross a wooden bridge then turn right over a second wooden bridge and go past locks as far as the mighty river. Return to the boatyard.

Picture: King Charles's House, Worcester.
AA Picture Library

2. To go north through Worcester, from the entrance to the boatyard, pass between the Grist Mill Boatyard (made of green corrugated iron) and the toilet block on a tarmac path.

3. Follow the canal towpath past the

Commandery for 2.5 miles as far as lock 7, bridge 15 (Binford Top Lock) near to Perdiswell Leisure Centre. After this the surface of the towpath soon deteriorates, becoming narrower, muddier, bumpier and more overgrown.

Picture: Worcester. *AA Picture Library*

Picture opposite: St Andrew's, Worcester. *AA Picture Library*

TWO RIDES ALONGSIDE THE RIVER SEVERN THROUGH WORCESTER

Worcester is a cathedral city and the bustling county capital of Worcestershire. This ride runs north and south from the bridge over the River Severn, which provides a green corridor through the heart of the city. The section to the north does a circuit around the outside of the race course.

NB. This ride is best avoided if there is a race meeting at Worcester.

Background and places of interest

(See Route 27)

Picture: Bridge over Severn, Worcester.
AA Picture Library

Starting Point: The long-term car park immediately next to the filling station, just over the river bridge heading away from the town centre. Follow signs for A44 Leominster over the bridge then immediately left.

Parking: As above.

Distance: 1 mile on the route going south; a 2-mile circuit of the race course.

Map: Ordnance Survey Landranger Sheet 150.

Hills: None.

Surface: Good, broad gravel tracks.

Roads and road crossings: The busy A44 can be crossed at the traffic lights near the car park.

Refreshments: Lots of choice in Worcester.

Cycle Hire: Available from Cadence Cycle Hire on Foregate Street Railway Station. Tel: 0905 613501.

Route Instructions:

1. Head south along the river following signs for Bromwick Road via Weir Lane. It is suggested you turn around and return where the track

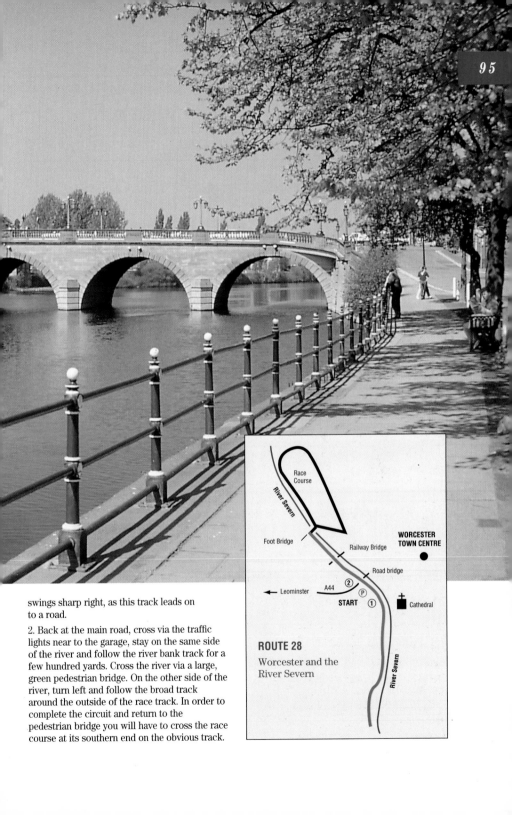

swings sharp right, as this track leads on
to a road.

2. Back at the main road, cross via the traffic
lights near to the garage, stay on the same side
of the river and follow the river bank track for a
few hundred yards. Cross the river via a large,
green pedestrian bridge. On the other side of the
river, turn left and follow the broad track
around the outside of the race track. In order to
complete the circuit and return to the
pedestrian bridge you will have to cross the race
course at its southern end on the obvious track.

Map labels

Race Course

River Severn

Foot Bridge

Railway Bridge

WORCESTER TOWN CENTRE

Road bridge

Leominster

A44

② P

START ①

Cathedral

River Severn

ROUTE 28
Worcester and the
River Severn

THE STRATFORD GREENWAY

(Southwest from Stratford-upon-Avon on a dismantled railway)

As a break from 'doing Shakespeare' you might well be pleased to get on to your bike and head out of Stratford into the countryside along the course of this dismantled railway. The route passes close to the race course, crossing the River Avon via a fine old iron bridge. The first 2.5 miles of the route are in excellent condition, the second half is slightly rougher.

Background and places of interest

Built in 1859 by the Oxford, Worcester & Wolverhampton Railway and later absorbed by the Great Western Railway, the line linked Stratford and the Midlands to Cheltenham and the Southwest. Finally, as part of British Rail, it carried the 'Cornishman' to and from the West Country until the line was closed in 1976.

● **Stratford-upon-Avon**

Renowned as the birthplace of Shakespeare, this well-preserved market town is a showcase of Tudor architecture, its broad streets lined with half-timbered houses. There is plenty to see in the town, but of particular interest to children might be the Teddy Bear Museum, with a collection of some of the most unusual teddy bears from around the world; the World of Shakespeare, with life-size tableaux re-creating sights and sounds of Shakespearean England, from the court of Elizabeth I to street slums; and the Stratford Butterfly and Jungle Safari, where hundreds of moths and butterflies fly among exotic plants trees and flowers.

Picture: Motor Museum, Stratford. *AA Picture Library*

Starting Point: The car park at the start of the track, southwest of Stratford near the race course. Follow signs for the A4390, which is Stratford's ring road/bypass between the A3400 from the south (Oxford) and the A3400 to the north (Henley-in-Arden).

Parking: As above.

Distance: 5 miles (10 miles round trip).

Map: Ordnance Survey Landranger Sheet 151.

Hills: None.

Surface: Good, broad, stone-based track. The 2.5 miles closer to Stratford are in excellent condition. The second half is slightly rougher.

Roads and road crossings: You will have to spend a short time on a quiet lane if you wish to visit the pub in Long Marston.

Refreshments: Masons Arms PH, Long Marston.

Route Instructions:
The route ends at a road by an industrial estate. If you wish to go to the pub, on your outward journey from Stratford, cross the road at Milcote car park, then at the second row of white-painted, upright railway sleepers by a line of telegraph poles, turn right. At the T-junction at the end of Wyre Lane, turn right for 200yds for the Masons Arms.

Picture: Garrick Inn, Stratford. *AA Picture Library*

CHESHIRE

Lyme Park, southeast of Manchester. Access from the A6 near Disley (between Stockport and Glossop). A National Trust property with 1,400 acres of parkland and a reasonably liberal attitude to cycling. You are allowed on all the tarmac roads and any of the broad stone-based tracks, unless a sign tells you otherwise. There is even a 5-acre site on an old quarry set by for the more adventurous mountain biker. Laminated signs throughout the park indicate where you are.

DERBYSHIRE/ SOUTH YORKSHIRE

Staveley to Killamarsh trail and Rother Valley Country Park. Access off A619 east of Chesterfield or A6135 southeast of Sheffield.

A 4-mile trail along a dismantled railway and a circuit of the lake in Rother Valley Country Park.

DERBYSHIRE

Carsington Water. Access off the B5035 between Ashbourne and Wirksworth. Signposted with brown-and-white Carsington Water signs. Britain's newest reservoir, opened in early 1993. Visitor Centre open every day from 10.00am, with exhibition, shops, restaurant, cafe, adventure playground and cycle hire (at the weekends) Tel: 0629 85478.

NOTTINGHAMSHIRE

Bestwood Country Park, north of Nottingham. Take either the A60 Mansfield road or the A611 Hucknall road out of Nottingham. A 400-acre park with tracks open for cycling. Tel: 0602 670042.

Picture: *Mike Williams*

NOTTINGHAMSHIRE

The Southwell Trail. Access off the A617
between Mansfield and Newark-on-Trent.
A 6-mile trail along a dismantled railway
between Southwell and Bilsthorpe, following the
Robin Hood Way for part of its length.

SHROPSHIRE

Nescliffe Hill Country Park, 9 miles northwest of
Shrewsbury off the A5 between the villages of
Nescliffe and Ruyton-XI-Towns. The 160-acre
park includes impressive woodland, an Iron Age
hillfort, panoramic views and the legendary
Humphrey Kynaston's cave. There is a
waymarked cycle route.

SHROPSHIRE

The Silkin Way. A 14-mile trail through Telford
using dismantled railways and dry canal beds.
Leaflet available from: Stirchley Grange,
Wrekin Countryside Wardens, Stirchley Road,
Telford TF3 1DY. Tel: 0952 590936.

LEICESTERSHIRE

Ashby Woulds Heritage Trail, 3 miles west of
Ashby-de-la-Zouch on the B5003 (southeast of
Burton Upon Trent). The 3-mile trail runs along
the course of a dismantled railway between the
villages of Moira and Measham. Parking at the
Moira Furnace car park, just off the B5003 to the
west of Moira. The Moira Blast Furnace is one
of the best preserved furnaces from the period
of the Napoleonic Wars.

Could be combined with:

a. The impressive ruins of Ashby castle in
Ashby-de-la-Zouch with its massive tower and
underground passage. Tel: 0530 413343.

b. Battlefield Steam Railway, Shackerstone.
Regular Sunday Steam service from mid-March
to October on a 9-mile round trip from
Shackerstone to Shenton. Museum and tea
room. Tel: 0533 871645.

c. Market Bosworth Visitor Centre. Exhibition
covering the Battle of Bosworth of 1485, the
final battle of the Wars of the Roses.
Film theatre, book and gift shop. Restaurant.
Battle trails. Open daily April to October.
Tel: 0455 290429.

d. Twycross Zoo, Twycross, Atherstone. Large
collection of animals, including many rare and
endangered species. Open daily all year.
Tel: 0827 880250.

Picture: *Stockfile*

Picture (top): *Stockfile*

Picture (above): *Nick Cotton*

LEICESTERSHIRE

Bradgate Park and Swithland Wood Estate, access off the A50 north of Leicester. Bradgate Park is an 850-acre historic deer park and Swithland Wood a mature broadleaf woodland of 146 acres. There is a traffic-free road which runs through the park where you can cycle, although it does get very busy with pedestrians during the summer and at the weekends. You will have to negotiate some unfriendly gates with your bicycle to get into the park. Could be combined with:

a. Snibston Discovery Park, Ashby Road, Coalville, (4 miles west of M1/Junction 22). Extensive hands-on science displays. The various galleries reflect Leicestershire's industrial heritage. Walk through a tornado! Open daily all year. Tel: 0530 813256.

b. Beacon Hill Country Park, Woodhouse Eaves. One of the highest points in Leicestershire, with a toposcope to identify features in the extensive views. Open all year during daylight hours.

WEST MIDLANDS

The Birmingham and Black Country Cycleway. The 14-mile towpath along the main line canal between Birmingham and Wolverhampton is gradually being improved for walkers and cyclists. You may find it useful to take an A-Z of Birmingham with you. A good leaflet is available from: British Waterways, Birmingham and Black Country Canals, Bradley Lane, Bilston, West Midlands WV14 8DW. Tel: 0902 409010.

The Forestry Commission owns many thousands of acres of land in the area covered by this book and has, by and large, adopted an enlightened approach to cycling in its woodlands. The broad rule of thumb is that you are allowed to ride on the hard, stone-based forestry roads which provide excellent opportunities for safe, family cycling. You are NOT allowed to cycle in the woodland away from these hard tracks and should pay attention to any signs which may indicate a temporary or permanent restriction on cycling (normally on walkers' trails or where forestry operations are in progress).

In some places, the forest authorities have even waymarked a trail for cyclists. However, open access is not universally the case, and in some woodlands you are only allowed on tracks where there is a statutory right of way, namely bridleways and byways.

This may all sound a little confusing, but the Forestry Commission is extremely helpful and normally has good reasons for restricting access. The forests are working environments where heavy machinery is often being used to fell or plant trees and whenever work is in progress there will be restrictions on recreational use.

A phone call or a letter to your local Forest Enterprise office should clarify the situation (addresses and phone numbers listed below). In order to simplify matters as much as possible, forestry areas have been divided into three categories:

(**A**) sites where a trail has been waymarked for cyclists
(**B**) sites where there is an open access policy (except for walkers' trails)
(**C**) sites where you are restricted to statutory rights of way

The best maps to use for exploring Forestry Commission woodland are the most up-to-date Ordnance Survey Pathfinder maps, scale 1:25,000, which tend to be reasonably accurate. PLEASE NOTE. It must be stressed that there are many different user-groups enjoying the woodlands, so courtesy and consideration should be shown at all times to walkers and horse riders. The fact that a bike can travel faster than a pedestrian does not give you any priority; indeed priority normally lies with the walker or the horse rider. Use a bell to give warning of your presence and say thank you to people who step aside for you.

(A) FORESTRY WITH WAYMARKED CYCLE TRAILS

Clipstone Forest, 4 miles east of Mansfield, on the B6030 just east of Old Clipstone. This 6-mile route is described in full in the main part of the book (Route 17). For a leaflet covering Clipstone Forest and other woodland in Sherwood Forest, send an SAE to: Forestry Commission, Forest Enterprise, Sherwood and Lincs Forest District, Edwinstowe, Mansfield, Notts NG21 9JL. Tel: 0623 822447.

FC1 Delamere Forest, east of Chester, Cheshire. Starts from the Forestry Commission Discovery Centre, Linmere, Delamere, just off the B5152, signposted from the A556 Chester-Northwich road. Cycle hire available 10.00am-6.00pm on weekends Easter to October and every day in July and August. Leaflet available by sending 60p plus SAE to: Forest Enterprise, Linmere, Delamere, Northwich, Cheshire CW8 2JD. Tel: 0606 882167.

FC2 Shropshire Woodland Trails:

(**a**) Two routes from Bury Ditches car park, 25 miles south of Shrewsbury and 5 miles south of Bishop's Castle off the B4385 (grid reference SO 334838).

(**b**) Three routes from Poles Coppice car park, 10 miles southwest of Shrewsbury along the A488, then turn off at Minsterley towards Habberley (grid reference SJ 386043).

For a leaflet for the above routes send £1.00 plus SAE to: Countryside Unit, Shropshire County Council, Leisure Services Department, Winston Churchill Building, Radbrook Road, Shrewsbury SY3 9BJ.

FC3 Hopton Mountain Bike Trail, 10 miles west of Ludlow on the A4113 then the B4385 northwest. The car park is on a minor road just to the west of Hopton Castle (grid reference SO 350779). For a laminated leaflet, resistant to water and mud, send 50p plus SAE to: Forestry Commission, Marches Forest District, Whitcliffe, Ludlow, Shropshire SY8 2HD.

Picture: *Stockfile*

FC4 Fineshade Wood, 12 miles west of Peterborough (southeast of Rutland Water). The car park is off the A43, 3 miles south from Duddington towards Corby (grid reference SP 980982). For leaflet send SAE to: Forest Enterprise, Northants Forest District, Top Lodge, Fineshade, Corby, Northants NN17 3BB.

(B) FORESTRY WITH OPEN ACCESS (EXCEPT FOR RESTRICTED PEDESTRIAN AREAS)

- **Sherwood area:**

1. Thieves Wood and Harlow Wood

2. Blidworth Wood and Haywood Oaks

Picture: *Stockfile*

3. Whitwell Wood

These woodlands all lie within an arc to the west of Mansfield. For a leaflet send SAE to: Forestry Commission, Forest Enterprise, Sherwood and Lincs Forest District, Edwinstowe, Mansfield, Notts NG21 9JL, or telephone 0623 822447 for details of restrictions.

NB Birklands (next to Sherwood Visitor Centre) has a general restriction to statutory bridleways only. The pack of leaflets produced by Nottinghamshire County Council, 'Nottinghamshire Cycle Routes' (see details on pages 108/109) contains a legal off-road ride in the area.

- **Northamptonshire area:**
1. Bourne Wood (north of Peterborough)
2. Fermyn Forest Walk (east of Corby)
3. Southey Wood (west of Peterborough)
4. Wakerley Great Wood (west of Peterborough)
5. Salcey Forest (southeast of Northampton)

For leaflets send SAE to Forest Enterprise, Northants Forest District, Top Lodge, Fineshade, Corby, Northants NN17 3BB, or telephone 078 083 394/5 for details of restrictions.

- **Around Birmingham:**
1. Cannock Chase (southeast of Stafford)
2. Wyre Forest (west of Kidderminster)
3. Woodland southwest of Ludlow

There are no leaflets produced covering these areas, but you may wish to phone the following numbers to find out about any developments:

Cannock Chase — Midlands Forest District, Rugeley. Tel: 0889 586593.

Wyre, Ludlow — Marches Forest District, Ludlow. Tel: 0584 874542.

(C) FORESTRY WHERE ACCESS IS RESTRICTED TO STATUTORY RIGHTS OF WAY

1. All forestry land in Derbyshire

2. Birklands near Edwinstowe in Sherwood Forest (adjoining the Visitor Centre) (See details in section [B] above)

The theory is that there are 2,000 miles of towpaths in England and Wales, offering flat, vehicle-free cycling. The reality is that only a fraction of the towpath network is suitable for cycling: the rest is too narrow, overgrown, muddy and rough. There is obviously much room for improvement and certain waterways boards, in conjunction with local authorities and the Countryside Commission, have made immense progress in improving towpaths for all user groups. However, even the areas which have a reasonable surface are often busy with anglers and walkers, so when cycling on canal towpaths, extra care and consideration is needed.

Within the book there are five rides on short sections of canal towpaths, one of which is close to a flight of locks for its scenic and architectural interest. For the rest of the canal network please refer to the map and to the addresses and phone numbers of the local waterways board covering your area. The authorities have undertaken a complete survey of the towpath network, abolished the system of permits and established much clearer guidelines about where you can and cannot cycle. The most up-to-date information can be obtained from your local waterways board.

The addresses and phone numbers are as follows:

• Cheshire
Pennine and Potteries Waterways, Top Lock, Church Lane, Marple, Stockport, Cheshire SK6 6BN. Tel: 061 427 1079.

• Leicestershire
(see Nottinghamshire)

• Northamptonshire
Grand Union Canal Central, The Stop House, The Wharf, Braunston NN11 7JQ. Tel: 0788 890666.

• Nottinghamshire
1. East Midlands Navigations, Mill Lane, Mill Gate, Newark, Nottinghamshire NG24 4TT. Tel: 0636 704481.

2. Grand Union Canal North, Trent Lock, Lock Lane, Long Eaton, Nottingham NG10 2FF. Tel: 0602 461017.

• Shropshire
Border Counties Waterways, Canal Office, Birch Road, Ellesmere SY12 9AA. Tel: 0691 622549.

• Staffordshire and Warwickshire
1. Trent and Mersey Canal, Fradley Junction, Alrewas, Burton-on-Trent DE13 7DN. Tel: 0283 790236.

2. Staffordshire and Shropshire Union Canals, Norbury Junction, Stafford ST20 0PN. Tel: 0785 284253.

• West Midlands
Birmingham and Black Country Canals, Bradley Lane, Bilston WV14 8DW. Tel: 0902 409010.

• Worcestershire
Worcester and Birmingham Canal, Brome Hall Lane, Lapworth, Solihull, West Midlands B94 5RB. Tel: 0564 784634.

Canal network of
Midlands & Peak District

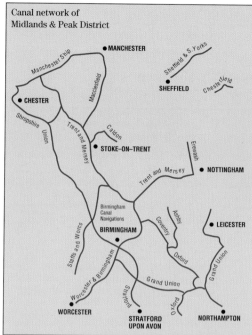

THE WATERWAYS CODE FOR CYCLISTS

1. Access paths can be steep and slippery — join the towing path with care.

2. Always give way to other people on the towing path and warn them of your approach. A 'hello' and 'thank you' mean a lot. Be prepared to dismount if the path is busy with pedestrians or anglers.

3. You must dismount and push your cycle if the path narrows, or passes beneath a low bridge or alongside a lock.

4. Ride at a gentle pace, in a single file, and do not bunch.

5. Never race — you have water on one side of you.

6. Watch out when passing moored boats — there may be mooring spikes concealed on the path.

7. Take particular care on wet or uneven surfaces, and don't worsen them by skidding.

8. Never cycle along towing paths in the dark.

9. Towing paths are not generally suitable for organised cycling events, but the local Waterways Manager may give permission.

10. If you encounter a dangerous hazard, please notify the Waterway Manager at the regional office.

Please remember you are responsible for your own and others' safety! You are only allowed to cycle the towing paths if you follow this code.

Picture: *Stockfile*

CHESHIRE

Cheshire Cycleway. A 135-mile tour following quiet country lanes wherever possible, visiting villages, stately homes and country parks. Available for 30p from: Dept of Heritage and Recreation, Cheshire County Council, Goldsmith House, Hamilton Place, Chester CH1 1SE.

HEREFORD AND WORCESTER

Cycle Route Guide to Hereford and Worcester. Ten leaflets for £1.00 plus 36p postage available from: Hereford and Worcester County Council, County Engineer and Planning Officer, County Hall, Spetchley Road, Worcester WR5 2NP. Tel: 0905 763763. Also available, free of charge, three cycle-route guides to North Worcestershire. Address as above.

LEICESTERSHIRE

Cycling around Leicestershire. A 140-mile route around the county on quiet country lanes.

Send large SAE to Countryside and Recreation Section, Planning and Transportation Department, Leicestershire County Council, County Hall, Glenfield, Leicester LE3 8RJ. Tel: 0533 657091. Also three leaflets, costing 15p each, with a total of nine routes around Rutland Water. They are called *Cycling around Rutland.* Address as above.

NORTHAMPTONSHIRE

Northamptonshire Cycle Tours. Three leaflets describing a total of five rides of between 6 and 21 miles. Send SAE to Northamptonshire Country Services, 9 Guildhall Road, Northampton NN1 1DP.

NOTTINGHAMSHIRE

a. Two packs of leaflets describing cycle rides in Nottinghamshire. The packs costs £1.50 each (plus 50p postage per pack) and are available from: The Rights of Way Section,

Nottinghamshire County Council, Trent Bridge House, Fox Road, West Bridgford, Nottingham NG2 6BJ. Tel: 0602 774483.

b. Two leaflets entitled *Dukeries Cycle Trails*, describing several short loops around Clumber, are available by sending an SAE to: Tourist Information Centre, Bassetlaw District Council, Public Library, Memorial Avenue, Worksop S80 2BP. Tel: 0909 501148.

PEAK DISTRICT

The Peak National Park produces a series of leaflets relating to rides and trails within the park. Send large SAE to:Peak National Park, Peak Park Joint Planning Board, Aldern House, Baslow Road, Bakewell, Derbyshire DE45 1AE. Tel: 0629 814321.

SHROPSHIRE

Shropshire County Council produces two leaflets: *The Corvedale Cycle Tour* (50p), a 27- or 40-mile route along quiet Shropshire lanes, starting from Ludlow and *Countryside and Woodland Cycle Trails* (75p) containing details of five shorter rides which are a mixture

of lanes and off-road tracks. Available from: Shropshire Books, Winston Churchill Building, Radbrook Centre, Radbrook Road, Shrewsbury, Shropshire SY3 9BJ. Tel: 0743 254043.

STAFFORDSHIRE

Cycle and See the Staffordshire Moorlands. Five leaflets describing rides of 20-30 miles. Send £2.20 to: The Leek Tourist Office, Market Place, Leek, Staffs ST13 5HH. Tel: 0538 381000.

WEST MIDLANDS

The Birmingham Cycling Project, 54 Allison St, Digbeth, Birmingham B5 5TH (Tel: 021 632 6753) produces a series of leaflets about cycling around Birmingham and the West Midlands. Send an SAE for a list of their titles.

OTHERS

The Cycling Project for the Northwest sells a whole range of leaflets, some of which overlap with the area covered by this book.

For a list of the titles on offer, send an SAE to: CPNW, Environmental Institute, Bolton Road, Swinton, Manchester M27 2UX.

Picture: *Mike Williams*

Local authorities are the obvious organisations to contact to find out what cycle routes exist locally, what plans there are for the future and for reporting any complaints you may have about the provision of cycle routes in your area. Their addresses are as follows:

CHESHIRE
Heritage and Recreation Service, Goldsmith House, Hamilton Place, Chester CH1 1SE. Tel: 0244 602483.

DERBYSHIRE
a. Planning and Highways, County Offices, Matlock DE4 3AG. Tel: 0629 580000.
b. Peak District National Park, Aldern House, Baslow Road, Bakewell DE45 1AE. Tel: 0629 814321.

HEREFORD AND WORCESTER
The Countryside Officer, County Hall, Spetchley Road, Worcester WR5 2NP. Tel: 0905 766899.

LEICESTERSHIRE
Countryside Section, Planning and Transportation Dept., County Hall, Glenfield, Leicester LE3 8RJ. Tel: 0533 657082.

NORTHAMPTONSHIRE
Northants Country Services, Countryside Centre, 9 Guildhall Road, Northampton NN1 1DP. Tel: 0604 237220.

NOTTINGHAMSHIRE
Countryside Services Dept, Trent Bridge House, Fox Road, West Bridgford NG2 6BJ. Tel: 0602 823823.

SHROPSHIRE
Countryside Service, Shropshire Leisure Services, Churchill Building, Radbrook Road, Shrewsbury SY3 9BJ. Tel: 0743 254004.

STAFFORDSHIRE
Countryside Access Officer, Staffs County Council, Martin Street, Stafford ST16 2LE. Tel: 0785 277244.

WARWICKSHIRE
Planning and Transport Dept, Shire Hall, Warwick CV34 4SX. Tel: 0926 412342.

For addresses of British Waterways Boards and Forestry Commission regional offices, please see the appropriate chapters.

THE CYCLISTS TOURING CLUB (CTC)
Cotterell House, 69 Meadrow, Godalming, Surrey GU7 3HS. Tel: 0483 417217.
Britain's largest cycling organisation, promoting recreational and utility cycling. The CTC provides touring and technical advice, legal aid and insurance, and campaigns to improve facilities and opportunities for all cyclists.

THE CYCLE CAMPAIGN NETWORK
c/o London Cycling Campaign, 3 Stamford Street, London SE1 9NT. Tel: 071 928 7220.
A clearing house for news and information among Britain's many local cycle campaigns, this group also acts as a watchdog, closely monitoring the progress of Bills in Parliament that could adversely affect the rights of cyclists and maintains links with similar organisations worldwide. Contact the CCN if you want to know where your nearest cycle campaign is or if you want to set up one yourself.

SUSTRANS
35 King Street, Bristol BS1 4DZ. Tel: 0272 268893.
A registered charity, Sustrans designs and builds systems for sustainable transport. It is best known for its transformation of old railway lines into safe, traffic-free routes for cyclists, pedestrians and wheelchair users. It often needs volunteer labour and the development of new routes is largely funded by individual subscribers.

Facing Picture: *Stockfile*